BRANDON MCKOY

The Business You Keep Avoiding

How To Build Long-Term Wealth As A Creative

First published by AskUncleBrandon LLC 2025

Cover Design by Lesia S.

All Scripture quotations, unless otherwise stated, are from the King James Version of the Bible.

First edition

ISBN: 979-8-218-88746-9

This book was professionally typeset on Reedsy.
Find out more at reedsy.com

Contents

EPIGRAPH

As I died, I came alive.

Much like King David did for his son and successor, Solomon, God gave me instructions for the next part in my life as the old part was dying. My instructions came from Jesus himself in Matthew 5:48,

1 And seeing the multitudes, he went up into a mountain: and when he was
set, his disciples came unto him: **2** And he opened his mouth, and taught
them, saying, **3** Blessed are the poor in spirit: for theirs is the kingdom of
heaven. **4** Blessed are they that mourn: for they shall be comforted. **5** Blessed
are the meek: for they shall inherit the earth. **6** Blessed are they which do
hunger and thirst after righteousness: for they shall be filled. 7 Blessed are
the merciful: for they shall obtain mercy. **8** Blessed are the pure in heart:
for they shall see God. **9** Blessed are the peacemakers: for they shall be
called the children of God. **10** Blessed are they which are persecuted for
righteousness' sake: for theirs is the kingdom of heaven. **11** Blessed are ye,
when men shall revile you, and persecute you, and shall say all manner of
evil against you falsely, for my sake. **12** Rejoice, and be exceeding glad: for
great is your reward in heaven: for so persecuted they the prophets which
were before you. **13** Ye are the salt of the earth: but if the salt have lost his
savour, wherewith shall it be salted? it is thenceforth good for nothing, but
to be cast out, and to be trodden under foot of men. **14** Ye are the light of
the world. A city that is set on an hill cannot be hid. **15** Neither do men light
a candle, and put it under a bushel, but on a candlestick; and it giveth light
unto all that are in the house. **16** Let your light so shine before men, that they
may see your good works, and glorify your Father which is in heaven. **17**
Think not that I am come to destroy the law, or the prophets: I am not come

to destroy, but to fulfil. **18** For verily I say unto you, Till heaven and earth
pass, one jot or one tittle shall in no wise pass from the law, till all be fulfilled.
19 Whosoever therefore shall break one of these least commandments, and
shall teach men so, he shall be called the least in the kingdom of heaven:
but whosoever shall do and teach them, the same shall be called great in the
kingdom of heaven. **20** For I say unto you, That except your righteousness
shall exceed the righteousness of the scribes and Pharisees, ye shall in no
case enter into the kingdom of heaven. **21** Ye have heard that it was said
of them of old time, Thou shalt not kill; and whosoever shall kill shall be
in danger of the judgment: **22** But I say unto you, That whosoever is angry
with his brother without a cause shall be in danger of the judgment: and
whosoever shall say to his brother, Raca, shall be in danger of the council: but
whosoever shall say, Thou fool, shall be in danger of hell fire. **23** Therefore if
thou bring thy gift to the altar, and there rememberest that thy brother hath
ought against thee; **24** Leave there thy gift before the altar, and go thy way;
first be reconciled to thy brother, and then come and offer thy gift. **25** Agree
with thine adversary quickly, whiles thou art in the way with him; lest at any
time the adversary deliver thee to the judge, and the judge deliver thee to the
officer, and thou be cast into prison. **26** Verily I say unto thee, Thou shalt
by no means come out thence, till thou hast paid the uttermost farthing. **27**
Ye have heard that it was said by them of old time, Thou shalt not commit
adultery: **28** But I say unto you, That whosoever looketh on a woman to lust
after her hath committed adultery with her already in his heart. **29** And if thy
right eye offend thee, pluck it out, and cast it from thee: for it is profitable
for thee that one of thy members should perish, and not that thy whole body
should be cast into hell. **30** And if thy right hand offend thee, cut it off,
and cast it from thee: for it is profitable for thee that one of thy members
should perish, and not that thy whole body should be cast into hell. **31** It
hath been said, Whosoever shall put away his wife, let him give her a writing
of divorcement: **32** But I say unto you, That whosoever shall put away his
wife, saving for the cause of fornication, causeth her to commit adultery:
and whosoever shall marry her that is divorced committeth adultery. **33**
Again, ye have heard that it hath been said by them of old time, Thou shalt

not forswear thyself, but shalt perform unto the Lord thine oaths: **34** But I
say unto you, Swear not at all; neither by heaven; for it is God's throne: **35**
Nor by the earth; for it is his footstool: neither by Jerusalem; for it is the city
of the great King. **36** Neither shalt thou swear by thy head, because thou
canst not make one hair white or black. **37** But let your communication be,
Yea, yea; Nay, nay: for whatsoever is more than these cometh of evil. **38** Ye
have heard that it hath been said, An eye for an eye, and a tooth for a tooth:
39 But I say unto you, That ye resist not evil: but whosoever shall smite thee
on thy right cheek, turn to him the other also. **40** And if any man will sue
thee at the law, and take away thy coat, let him have thy cloak also. **41** And
whosoever shall compel thee to go a mile, go with him twain. **42** Give to
him that asketh thee, and from him that would borrow of thee turn not thou
away. **43** Ye have heard that it hath been said, Thou shalt love thy neighbour,
and hate thine enemy. **44** But I say unto you, Love your enemies, bless them
that curse you, do good to them that hate you, and pray for them which
despitefully use you, and persecute you; **45** That ye may be the children of
your Father which is in heaven: for he maketh his sun to rise on the evil and
on the good, and sendeth rain on the just and on the unjust. **46** For if ye love
them which love you, what reward have ye? do not even the publicans the
same? **47** And if ye salute your brethren only, what do ye more than others?
do not even the publicans so? **48** Be ye therefore perfect, even as your Father
which is in heaven is perfect.

INTRODUCTION

Why Your Calling Keep Disrupting Your Plans

Sometimes God asks you to simply be obedient because He knows you can be trusted to listen to His voice. He guides you in ways that allow what you need to fall into place, rather than revealing everything to you outright. If God handed you the full plan for your life all at once, you might feel overwhelmed, give up too soon, or try to change or rush the process. But it's the timing of what God is doing—piece by piece—that creates the abundance of spiritual, emotional, and financial wealth. The timing of God's order is what makes room for the miracles.

PART I - THE INNER BREAKING

What Is This Part Doing?

AN OVERVIEW

This chapter is your spiritual awakening narrative. Beyond your personal transformation, this chapter talks about the *death of the self that resists God.* Here we describe:

- The moment your old identity died
- Your frustration with obedience
- The pain of being misunderstood
- The internal war between control and surrender
- Jesus as the model of misunderstood obedience
- Why your community can't perceive your assignment
- Why obedience always separates you from what's familiar

Psychologically, this chapter is about **identity rupture**. We outline the moment when who you used to be cannot survive the calling on your life.

Emotionally, it confronts our fear of obedience, fear of being misunderstood, and fear of losing control.

Spiritually, it lays the foundation that trust is the first currency of wealth. We must learn to trust God fully before money, strategy, and opportunities.

Chapter One: Genesis – Start Here

I could mark the exact day that my old self completely died and my new self was completely formed. One could assume that was the moment all the prayers I'd been praying finally got answered. And honestly, I assumed the same thing. I experienced a lot of warfare and often felt like I was lost and betrayed by God in moments of believing something specific to happen. But it didn't happen the way I expected it to go.

I was angry with God. I hated being anointed and called. I hated the fact that I was obedient to God, I sacrificed, heard his voice and gave my all and still nothing happened. Even when receiving the release, I still found myself angry with God because in my obedience to Him I still had to deal with the weight of the decisions I made on Earth while being obedient to His will in heaven. I felt like I was living a suffering life here on Earth while having to find solace in a seemingly fictional place that I could not see nor touch. However, on this journey, I recognized the reason I kept hitting roadblocks was my need for wanting control.

People around me couldn't see nor understand my obedience to the voice of God. I struggled with understanding. How could I hear from God and the people that love me and God has sent to surround me for support can't understand my vision? Even the people around me in my closest circle did not understand my level of faith, nor could they connect to see or feel the magnitude of belief I have in God. Perceptibly, I had the power to move and remove myself from the situation that I was in, but it seemed like I found myself powerless. To them, it showed as a disbelief within myself and my own power. I found myself misunderstood. And it was at this point that I knew I had finally unlocked the mind of Jesus.

Jesus was a man who lived in reality, but in turn, many times, He was misunderstood. Jesus was misunderstood because of His obedience to His Father's voice. From birth, Jesus was destined for an assignment greater than himself. As he came to terms with this assignment and the many steps it would take to complete it, Jesus knew that His mind and belief in God were the most important things to His journey. One could assure and confirm that on His journey, Jesus became frustrated, tired, irritated, annoyed, worn thin, and completely fed up. But it was His life that had to be used as an example for what trusting the Father *looks* like. Ultimately, it was His outward display of pain in his death that demonstrated what trusting God *feels* like. In all, Jesus knew His mind had to stay conditioned and in order because of 1) His Surroundings and 2) His Confidence.

1. Jesus knew He had to be an example amongst people who did not fully trust God. Believers, non-believers, and enemies questioned him; challenged His beliefs and authorities; doubted His power and strength. However, Jesus knew He had to look crazy to fulfill the visions that God showed him. He knew He had to be radical to reach heights that seemed they were not attainable. Jesus knew that the darkness was necessary for Him to become what people needed him to be.
2. Jesus knew that His confidence and the way He lived His life, trusting the Father, would be used to minister to someone else. He knew that His confidence in God had to be the example of what Faith truly is. His mindset had to consistently be in tune with God. Therefore, His actions, even when misunderstood, represented Him following the voice of God rather than following what seemingly made sense to people.

Luke 2:41-50 is a scripture that outlines the experience of Jesus' childhood. As a 12-year-old, Jesus was misunderstood by his parents. Mary and Joseph, Jesus' parents, lost Him while on a trip. After looking everywhere in the area they had traveled, they finally found Jesus in a temple. Jesus is found speaking with the Teachers of the temple. When found, His parents were confused by his statement, "Did you not know that I must be about My Father's business?" While confused, His parents went on continuing to support him. They continued to raise him and be his guide until He was a man.

Mary and Joseph did not understand why Jesus was not found engaging in the expectation of a 12-year-old boy, but operating as a vessel amongst older men with wisdom. He was found sitting at the table amongst people who could pour into him beyond where He was at, but where He was going. What Mary and Joseph failed to grasp was that even at a young age, Jesus understood His assignment to minister and serve people.

We must mimic our life, striving to be like God in this manner. Early on in our walks of Christ and trusting God *fully,* we must consistently communicate that our obedience and alignment with the word of God is our divine mission.

In your journey of trusting God fully, you will be misunderstood by the people who raised you. They have seen you grow and helped you get to the place where you are. However, at times, your belief goes beyond what *they* are able to see for you. Note, what God is telling *you* to do is for *you*. Therefore, the people who raised you, whether it be spiritually, through childhood, mentorship, or elsewhere, will never understand your assignment and obedience to God's voice because it is not for them to understand. The people who raised you, supported you, and guided you in the past saw when you were broken. At times, your belief in God and fully trusting him breaks them. Your obedience to God breaks the people you love because they do not know how to fix the situation you are in. Unintentionally, they are upset, concerned, and ultimately confused because they want to be God for you. Naturally, the ones who raised you, supported you, and those you still rely on do not understand why you make the decisions you do. They stress themselves because they do not know how to be your saviour. Your responsibility in these moments is to remind them that you trust in God fully. Remind those who will misunderstand you that you are about your father's business. Remind them that your obedience is going to be an example to their part in your story of how trusting God became the answer to situations nobody *but God* could pull you through. Remind them that it is okay for you to be uncomfortable for a while if it means that God is pleased with your obedience.

John 3:1-10, Jesus is having a discussion with Nicodemus. Jesus says to him, "Except a man be born again, he cannot see the kingdom of God." Nicodemus responds, asking Jesus, "How can a man be born again if he is old? Does he have to climb back into his mother's womb?" It is here that Jesus is misunderstood by people who needed help from him. Jesus did not lash out or blame; He simply elaborated on His father's business. What Nicodemus did not realize is that Jesus was speaking of a spiritual rebirth, not physical.

Fully trusting God means that some people who still need help from you will not understand where the source of your resources comes from. However, they will reap the benefits of your suffering to God's will. It is not your responsibility to blame them for not understanding your assignment; however, you must show them the way of which you speak. Show them what it looks like to trust God *fully* and receive blessings that even those around can benefit from.

In scripture, there are also many times when Jesus is not understood, because of His timing in a predicament. In John 11:1-44, Lazarus is very sick. His sisters, Mary and Martha, call for Jesus to heal him. When Jesus heard that Lazarus was seemingly on his deathbed, He stayed two days where He was before arriving. By verse 21, Mary and Martha are quite irritated with Jesus, and they begin to blame Him, because their brother had died within those two days. While blaming Him, they had not known that out of obedience to

God, Jesus already knew and declared that "This sickness is not unto death, but for the glory of God, that the Son of God might be glorified thereby" in verse 4. Jesus was not late to Lazarus; He was in perfect timing to raise him from the dead by verse 44.

You will be misunderstood because of your obedience to God. In situations where it seemed as if you just would have done what was expected of you by people, then the outcome would have been different. Doing what people expect you to do over being obedient to God's specific instructions is what produces unnecessary struggle for you. You have to break the mindset of letting the expectation of people define your level of obedience to God. Our relationship with God must be a reflection of Christ's marriage to the church. The wedding vow speaks, "forsaking all others, be faithful to him/her as long as you both shall live." This vow in marriage not only refers to the romantic and sexual relationships with others; however, you must also forsake your obedience to others' assumptions of your behavior. Some assume that because you submitted to their control and order in the past, you will do it again. When you shift your mindset to fully trust God and be obedient to his voice *only*, that's when he has the room to speak life into you. This is why spiritual fasting works.

When you fast, you choose something that you are sacrificing and removing from yourself, and pair that removal with intentional prayer. Just as natural fasting, the process of removing an entity and being intentional about your behavior while that entity is removed allows space for a presence to operate more effectively. You have to make room for God to speak by removing other voices.

God gives you the plan for your life, the answer to your question, the escape route, the person to marry, the job to apply for, the time to quit, the turn to take, and so much more, when you remove things that have space in your mind. Your mindset being changed is the first step in God producing what you desire from Him.

In the Bible, God strategically lays out principles for us to follow. In explaining those principles, God gives us parables or stories that lay out how these principles work. Fortunately, God also allows these stories, parables, and examples to demonstrate what would happen if these principles are applied wrong, out of context, or completely ignored. In the case that we may miss it, God sends messengers who clearly outline the mindset He would like for us to have and complete our assignments.

There are Angelic messengers such as Gabriel who delivered key messages to Daniel, Zecharriah, and Mary about Jesus' birth. There are also human messengers, our Prophets, Pastors, and leaders, such as Moses who led Israel; Elijah & Elisha; Paul, Peter, John; John the Baptist, and so on. However, if we still did not heed the letters, wisdom, and lectures of those, God provided us with an ultimate messenger whose life was made to be an example of His Word made flesh.

With all of these examples, how is it that we still miss how God wants us to think? Here's how:

Being aligned with God, in tune with the Holy Spirit, and striving to live a life like Jesus is our focus. However, we become frustrated and struggle to be obedient to the messages we receive from God, because we have decided the message we want for ourselves is more important. When we decide that our claim and principles are more important than God's voice, we leave no space for God to be God for us. In turn, we become frustrated by walking *away* from what God said we were supposed to walk *through*.

Second, in our obedience to God's voice and principles, He reminds us that we are not striving toward what we want; however, His love allows us to experience the challenges necessary to produce what we need.

Principles are universal. If it works in one area, it will work in any other area. Consider Newton's First Law: an object at rest stays at rest; an object in motion stays in motion. No matter how you apply this principle to any object, the same laws will apply. Consider gravity; what goes up must come down. Any object that goes up in gravity *will* come down. So, how is it that God provides multiple examples, communicated multiple ways, from multiple people to be obedient to his instruction, yet, when it comes to following the principles of God to simply trust him, we make it complicated?

When God says, "Trust Me." that is not a suggestion to be customized. It's a principle — fixed, final, and not up for personal editing. Adding your doubts doesn't weaken His word; it just shows you're trying to insert your limitations into His limitless power. We trust God and follow his principles, right up to it being inconvenient for us. You being uncomfortable, looking out of place, having nothing but your trust in God, is exactly where He wants you to be. To note, **GOD DOES NOT WANT YOU TO BE BROKE** or broken; however, you have to break your old mindset of assuming your limitations in order to allow God to be limitless for you.

If you are going on the journey of creating spiritual, emotional, and financial wealth, you must trust God fully. The moment you insert doubt, fear, anxiety, or anything that is not what God told you to do, you are the hold up to your wealth release. You must take a spiritual journey *first* to align yourself with God and the principles He has designed for us to live by. From then on, use the spirit of God to guide you in healing your emotional alignment with his word and your obedience. From then, when your spirit and emotions are aligned with obedience to God, it frees your mind to receive strategies about how to build financial wealth. Ultimately, by consulting with the spirit of God and allowing our emotions to be tamed by God's will, we create a path that is aligned with a principle for us to thrive in spiritual, emotional, and financial wealth that is sustained and not threatened.

Chapter One A: Why Faith Keeps Feeling Like a Gamble

Any story in the bible, before God blesses anyone, He changes their mindset first. In order to obtain success you first have to believe that what you want is attainable and realistic for you.

The authorship of Hebrews is officially anonymous—the text itself does not name a writer, unlike many New Testament letters. Nevertheless, the letter is a sermon on endurance and perseverance. Hebrews 11:1 "Now faith is the substance of things hoped for; the evidence of things not seen."

What we are going to do is break down this scripture so that we understand its full meaning and how it relates to our life and obedience to God.

A lot of times it's quite irritating to hear preachers, believers, Bible talkers and Bible teachers discuss this scripture. Early in my life I always thought, how am I supposed to believe in Jesus Christ, be his child, and he says that he loves me, yet I'm supposed to have Faith in something that I can't see? Here's how:

NOW FAITH...(Here in the present future...)

The first two words of Hebrews 11:1 *"Now Faith"* gives understanding that the way God operates is never based in the past or trying to use your past to determine if He is going to bless you or not. "Now Faith" is referencing eternity. Eternity neither exists in the past nor the future, so, where does eternity exist? The Present. *"Now Faith"* is the present future where we exist in real time.

...IS THE SUBSTANCE... (...is the way someone stands under the point...)

Sub means under. Stance describes the way someone stands on a point. In our journey of endurance and perseverance, what is the point we should stand on? The point we should stand on is *"Now Faith."* As the scripture says *"Now Faith"* is the way someone stands under the point. The point you are standing on with your "Now Faith" is hope.

...OF THINGS HOPED FOR...(...of things we cannot see or have never seen..)

Things of hope are the things we can not see and the evidence of things we have never seen. Hope is an outcome that is not visible. Therefore, *"Now Faith"* is the way we stand under a point of things we can not see and have never seen.

THE EVIDENCE?

The evidence is what present thing is happening that creates the attainability and realistic nature that what we cannot see is already done. It has already happened. In other words, what we choose to see now shows that what we're hoping for is already real, even if we can't see it yet. So, what's the evidence? The evidence is YOU. Your life and the way you believe is the proof that what you are believing for is possible.

So, in full translation, Hebrews 11:1 would read as such:

Here in the present future, the point *you* stand on, the things *you* want and desire but cannot see or have ever seen, are realistic and attainable before you see it with your own two eyes.

Our life and how we live it in real time must be a living example that the things we want and desire from God are going to happen. We desire outcomes that are rooted in financial gain; however, the life we live in aligning our spirit, emotions, and finances with the principles of God is what is the evidence of wealth being attainable and realistic for us. And the way that we know our desires are aligned with God's is by connecting our mindset with the word of God. When your mindset and beliefs are aligned with the word of God, it is what proves that the attainability of wealth is real.

The proof of evidence in God being able and actively preparing you to receive spiritual, emotional, and financial wealth is your mindset. If you believe that it is attainable, then it is. You must choose to consistently believe and trust God so that the wealth you desire is not limited by any means outside of God's order. Thus, your spiritual, emotional, and financial wealth reaches its full, maximized potential.

Imagine a straight line. Your mindset of believing that God is able to do what you ask and desire is the straight line. The only way the line bends, curves, breaks, or is torn is by your wavering belief that what God said will happen, will come to pass. A simple principle of God—what you say and believe is possible to come to pass. Proverbs 18:21 "Death and Life are in the Power of the Tongue." Your belief creates your reality. Therefore, if you believe it's attainable, it will become real for you. Believe that the Power of God is real, and you being Biblically aligned with God's principles works! The moment you begin to speak or believe anything outside of God being the almighty, powerful, and able to fulfill your needs is when you have created a reality that your doubt is stronger than God. If God said it, believe it.

Chapter One B: Wealth Isn't Money

Wealth is defined as an abundance of valuable possession or money; a plentiful supply of a desirable thing.

Psalm 37:4 "Delight thyself also in the LORD: and he shall give thee the desires of thine heart." While commonly taught and preached, it is crucial that we understand the context of this scripture. King David is encouraging Faith when the wicked seem to prosper. Culturally, it is always quickly stated that God will give you the desires of your heart. This is true; however, the first part of the scripture instructs us on how to posture ourselves in order to *receive* the desires of our heart. Delighting yourself in the Lord involves exploring intimacy with God.

Spiritual Wealth

We are afraid of the word 'intimacy' because of its perceived association to be exclusively a discussion of sex. However, intimacy deals with the closeness and familiarity of self or self and other(s). Delighting yourself in the Lord requires that you have a close and familiar relationship with God. Like anything else, in order to become close and familiar, you must spend time with that entity. Anything in this world is retrievable with the exception of time. No human can acquire time that has already passed. Therefore, in time, we must be intentional about how we are choosing to be familiar in our relationships daily.

Being intimate with God involves you getting in His face daily in order to align yourself with His plan for your life. The way to align ourselves with God daily is by praying. Pray throughout all times of the day. It does not have to be fancy, elaborate, or use difficult language. Talk to God as if you are talking to your friend. Tell Him hello; acknowledge how powerful He is and what He is able to do; from then, confess your actions, wrong-doings, or short-comings; thank Him for His actions and ability to cleanse and save you from things you know or may have not known were a hindrance to you; then, end your prayer with asking for whatever specific things you need from God or desire.

Now, every prayer will not sound the same. Some prayers are ones of desperation, where the only words we can put together are "GOD HELP!" If we are aligned with God, communicating with Him, and spending time with Him every day, every request we make to Him, He answers.

It is debated in theological concepts that God will find us where we are according to His permissive will. The opposing view states that God operates in His Perfect or sovereign will. The perfect or sovereign will is what God intends or decrees to happen according to His divine purpose.

God does not force you to love Him. He gives you the choice to choose Him. All through human nature, it is we, people, humans, believers, non-believers, and so on who display the pattern of rejecting God and blaming Him for forsaking us. As early as Adam and Eve in Genesis 3, Adam blames God for giving him the woman who disobeyed the order He told Adam to enforce. The Israelites in the wilderness constantly complained and disobeyed God by worshipping a golden calf, yet when they were frustrated, they blamed God for the reason they were falling by the sword.

As humans, we have to be honest and real by recognizing the patterns in ourselves. All throughout the Bible, God gives people simple instructions, and they fail at upholding them. In turn, the sins they commit opened portals for destruction to enter. In Genesis 19:7, God told Lot and his wife, "Flee for your lives! Don't look back..." With simple instructions to move forward, Lot's wife turned into a pillar of salt because of her disobedience in sin.

Building an intimate relationship with God can not happen if you position yourself to be in defense against Him. His permissive will only takes place when you sin, and the divine will has to change for you to learn how to grow up. Until that time, God uses the intentional decisions you make in Him, allowing you to choose Him, and makes them work for your good. This is why delighting yourself in the Lord is crucial *before* He gives you the desires of your heart. You have to create an environment where He is welcomed and familiar with your face so that when the divine will is released to you–you don't taint it with your actions that are not aligned with God.

Naturally, humans rebel and sin. It is a humanitarian pattern for people to do wrong. Therefore, the scripture informs us to seek God daily in order to remain intimate with Him. If we are consistently seeking God's face for more, the desire of his divine will becomes our desire. So, delighting yourself in the Lord is an absolute non-negotiable for Him to release to you what the desires of your heart should be.

We become discouraged by God not fulfilling the desires of our heart as He promised. However, like any other human who blamed God for their disobedience, we failed to delight ourselves in the Lord *first*.

We must become wealthy in the spiritual relationship that we have with God. Spiritual alignment is spiritual wealth.

Not out of judgment, but an aware curiosity, who considers how God feels? Who prays for God? I often ask myself the question and ponder deeply, how is it that believers and even non-believers expect and ask for so much and have so little required of them, yet have a big return? If prayer alone were the answer to getting everything that God intended for us without any work or action, we would all have everything that we ask for.

Prayer is the communication of our desire to fulfill a request that God is already knowing of us to receive; however, there has to be formal contact made in order to allow any spiritual entity the access to operate in a realm from which it does not inherently derive from. Spirits have to be invited and given permission to enter into the Earthly realm. Prayer to God invites His spirit into the Earthly realm on our behalf.

Our trust in God must not be limited. Trusting God must happen in totality. However, when we do not trust God to do the greatest work in our lives, He has to reset our beliefs and mindset to trust in Him the right way. Most times, God has to break us all the way down to build us back up. It is at this moment that we finally submit to trusting God fully, because our trust in God is the only thing we are able to rely on.

When we have money, relationships, consistency, and resources, we can lose focus on trusting God completely due to feeling comfortable. Yes, we may experience some hardships, but God is not satisfied with you praying and talking to Him once you have a problem. If you are going to fully submit to God, He wants your full attention and reliance. Therefore, if you do not submit to His will the right way, He will strip your money, relationships, consistency, and resources for Him to be the sole reliant source of your life.

Spiritual wealth is being able to recognize and respond to God even when you don't fully understand what He's doing. Sometimes God will tell you to be obedient because He already knows you're capable of hearing His voice. Your obedience becomes the doorway through which He aligns the things you need. God, being the source, provides resources, connections, and opportunities that prompt your survival without having to explain every detail to you. While we may not understand, obedience is God's way of preparing you for what you've prayed for, without overwhelming you with the full picture. God moves in steps and increments we do not understand; however are beneficial for us. It is crucial to be obedient, because when we are not, we are delaying the plan for actions that are to follow our initial step.

If God gave you His entire plan up front, you would either quit out of fear or try to alter, accelerate, or control it. And God knows that. God knows you. So instead, God reveals His plan in pieces, in rhythms, and in His divine timing. It's the timing of what God is doing in your life and the process of how you are getting there that creates spiritual, emotional, and financial wealth.

Timing is the language of God's miracles. Magic depends on illusion, but miracles depend on timing, process, and obedience. Many times, we expect God to be magical. We want to perceive and suddenly appear at an outcome that is favorable for us. There are no principles that exist where any percentage of an outcome derives from zero percent of an input. You have to put in work to receive the outcome from God.

So, what's the difference between just doing work and actually doing work God tells you to do? Aligning yourself with God and His principles in the Bible allows the work that you do to be inclusively beneficial for a supernatural outcome being produced. When you do not consult with God, you can end up wasting time preparing and investing in areas that are not of your benefit. When you are not aligned with God, you can end up making mistakes and hitting dead ends that were preventable had you consulted with a source before engaging. Additionally, consulting with God gives you a layer of safety and direction for realignment if you lose your way. In other words, yes, you can do it on your own, but without proper guidance from the Holy Spirit, you will work harder to receive less than half of the result.

Emotional Wealth

While most of the ideas you have been taught about wealth surround money, it is not the fullest potential of how to thrive according to God's word. Now, we could just stick any category in front of the word 'wealth' and say that we're building in that area. But, for any area that we desire to build and thrive, it must begin with an awareness of our mindset, then execution of a plan that we create or choose to follow. In all, nothing happens if we ourselves do not feel like it. As people, we only do what we feel like doing. Even for the things we say we do not feel like doing, we end up doing them because we feel that the consequence of not doing it is greater than our resistance.

Wealth must be redefined in our mind in order to obtain it in truth. If your mind is not positioned to receive wealth, naturally, you will resist it. The reason you resist wealth is because you feel that the consequences of not obtaining it are greater than you actually becoming wealthy. For those who say, "That's Not Me." Consider why you have not pursued the journey of wealth early in your life. This is not to blame you; however, if we are going to build wealth in truth, we must break the conditioned emotions of poverty in our mindset. We do not pursue wealth early in our lives, because we are taught that we must stay little before we can grow. So, we spend our entire education career and experiences around staying in marginalized markets with caps for income. We are taught that you must work your way up to be truly successful. In so, we aim to be the best of the bottom instead of shooting toward the top and landing further up. We are taught that you must grind, sacrifice, and burnout in order to build wealth. That is not true. We are taught that you need permission to rise. People wait to be chosen, approved, validated, or certified. We are taught that we must thrive in diminutiveness, because if we receive increase too fast, it makes us not humble. That is an untruth designed to keep people small and working for others without growth.

Wealth is built by people who learn to choose themselves. You must make a conscious decision to be wealthy and stay wealthy. Some people pursue the benefits of wealth over having wealth itself. And guess what? That's okay too! It is not a sin nor is it a crime to pursue and want wealth. Most of us were taught that desiring wealth is selfish. We grow up hearing that wealth makes you greedy. That is not true. What truly makes you greedy is poverty in always finding a short-term way to survive over a long-term way to thrive.

People in poverty and poor mindsets are hyper-focused on lack. They have been taught to be aware of not receiving too much, but never told to be aware of always staying too little. When you're in survival mode, your brain is wired to prioritize safety, comfort, and immediate relief. That constant internal alarm leaves no room for long-term vision, creativity, or generosity. Survival steals mental freedom.

When you're not living in wealth, your brain works overtime to keep you stable. When you are not living in wealth, you search for nurturing, comfort, and anything that brings temporary relief. This is how we become addicted to substances, sports, sexual activity, spending, and more. Temporary relief is not the same as real mental freedom. We have to free our minds from repeating cycles that keep us stuck. We must recondition ourselves to deny short-term solutions so that we can achieve long-term transformation. The mind cannot expand when it's trapped in survival mode.

If this has been your mindset, it's okay. You don't need to blame yourself; you were trained to stay in mental poverty. But you *can* change.

Don't try, just do it.

Change begins by understanding wealth as more than dollars and currency.

Real wealth begins with being able to thrive in your emotions.

Emotional wealth is the foundation that allows spiritual and financial wealth to grow. It's the inner stability, clarity, and self-belief that frees your mind from survival mode so you can finally see opportunities instead of obstacles. When you build emotional wealth, you create the internal conditions necessary for financial wealth to not only arrive—but stay.

Emotional wealth is the internal mindset that controls your execution. While we may feel like it is money that motivates us or the Spirit of God, we only execute our actions because we feel like it. In so, the level of emotional wealth determines the quality of our life. If your quality of life is unstable, your financial success is directly threatened.

People wonder why millionaires and billionaires commit suicide. It is because your emotional wealth must coincide with your financial abundance. Those who live in abundance have learned to condition their minds to receive increase. They understand that abundance is not only a financial state but also a mental one. However, when a person has not positioned themself spiritually and emotionally for growth, the weight of abundance can become overwhelming. Many discover that having too much money without direction creates pressure rather than freedom. Purpose anchors your emotional life, giving direction and stability even during difficult seasons. When your actions align with your values, you generate a steady sense of fulfillment that money can't buy. Wealth without purpose often leads to confusion, restlessness, and a sense of emotional imbalance.

Sometimes, if our emotions are not aligned, we end up using our newfound financial increase to satisfy old emotions.

When money exists only to satisfy personal desires, it eventually loses its meaning. At some point, your desires run out, and your purchases no longer bring fulfillment. Once you reach that point, the question becomes, what comes next?

God has not designed wealth and abundance for us to go through a constant life cycle of gaining and losing. For those who seek purpose *after their financial increase* risk the temptation of believing that abundance is a curse. Abundance and financial increase being a curse is not true. True abundance requires more than the accumulation of money. It requires clarity, intention, and internal alignment. To acquire and sustain abundance, your spirit, mind, physical body, and actions must become one. If they do not, you risk unnecessary temptation that sends you backward in a place of lack.

To move forward, you must create an emotional and spiritual response to your wealth. You need a roadmap that guides your financial intention and connects your resources to a purpose beyond yourself. This roadmap helps you focus on impact, growth, contribution, and long-term fulfillment. When your mind, values, and intentions are aligned with your financial life, abundance becomes a tool for creation rather than a source of pressure.

The Core Pillars of Emotional Wealth

A. *Self-Awareness*

Emotional wealth begins with the ability to notice your inner world with clarity rather than judgment. The more accurately you can name what you feel, the more power you have to choose your responses. You have to be able to name what resistance to self-awareness causes your growth to fail.

Self-awareness allows us to separate our feelings and emotions from the emotions of others around us. Sometimes we believe things about ourselves because of the emotions of the people around us. For example, why do so many people believe that snakes, spiders, and mice are scary? Most people have never personally been harmed by any of these creatures, nor do they know someone who has. Yet the people around us often transfer their emotions and beliefs, and over time, we absorb them as our own. Without ever experiencing danger ourselves, we begin to believe that snakes, spiders, and mice are frightening simply because others have taught us to feel that way. This happens even though humans are bigger, stronger, wiser, and far more capable of communication than these small animals. In truth, most snakes, spiders, and mice pose very little threat to humans. Still, many people carry a deeply rooted fear of them based on the emotions and reactions of those around them. Self-awareness means recognizing that these creatures are actually more afraid of us than we are of them. They do not have authority over us. Instead, we have far more power, understanding, and control than they were ever designed to have over us.

Self-awareness is recognizing what your beliefs and biases are. While some people may say, "Well, I'm not biased to anything," that is untrue. It is a natural part of our existence to be biased. Due to pain and trauma we have experienced, society has deemed bias as a negative tool that specific groups use to marginalize others into an unfair circumstance. However, bias is simply based on what you believe, the thing you deny. Bias is what you do not accept. In becoming self-aware, you must recognize what narratives, beliefs, and conditions you do not accept. If you don't accept it, then you are biased against it. If you do accept it, you are biased towards it.

You must consistently stay self-aware in order to grow.

B. Emotional Regulation

Regulation is control that is set based on a standard. Concerning your emotional wealth, regulation is not about suppressing emotions, but creating enough internal space to respond instead of react. Reacting is providing an immediate action with the intent to affect an outcome. When you are not self-aware of your actions or the outcomes they create, your reactions can cause more harm than help. Because reacting happens instantly, the focus is not on resolution. Instead, your behavior is driven by the beliefs and assumptions you have already formed about the situation you are experiencing. This is why many people jump, scream, or panic when they are startled. These reactions are conditioned behaviors that interpret any amount of darkness, uncertainty, or surprise as a threat. The body and mind move automatically, without evaluating whether the situation is actually dangerous.

Responding, however, is different. Responding requires self-awareness. It allows you to pause long enough to determine whether something is truly hurtful or harmful. Once you recognize what is happening, you can assess the level of threat or discomfort and choose how to address it. From there, you can develop a strategy that is specifically tailored to influence the outcome.

The main difference is that reacting is automatic and emotionally driven, while responding is conscious, thoughtful, and aligned with your desired outcome. Reacting comes from instinct. Responding comes from healthy self-awareness.

C. Self-Worth & Inner Security

Emotional wealth grows when your sense of value comes from within instead of depending on external validation. Our need to be validated is natural; however, our emotional wealth being in the hands of others who are not emotionally regulated is dangerous.

Seeking validation of ourselves from others who have not done the work to become emotionally regulated is dangerous because their beliefs that determine your worth are built on misunderstandings and untruth. In so doing, they make you believe that your worth is "not enough," because they do not understand where you are going. Healing the internal "not enough" story creates a stable emotional foundation that cannot be taken away. We must find worth within ourselves without depending on the validation of others.

D. Relationships & Emotional Connection

Emotional wealth flourishes in strong, healthy relationships built on honesty, reciprocity, and boundaries. It is okay to tell people "no" or "I can't do that." Those who accept your "no" and move forward with the relationship without attempting to manipulate your change in response are highly valued relationships. Any relationship you are in that respects your decision-making and boundaries is one that supports your emotional wealth. If there is a relationship you are in that is aware of your boundaries or decision-making, and they continue to allow your behavior to cause negative outcomes, those are low-value relationships. If you are in a relationship where someone is fully aware of your boundaries and the way you make decisions, yet they continue to allow your behavior to lead to negative outcomes, that is a low-value relationship. High-value relationships support growth, accountability, and mutual responsibility, not cycles of harm or unhealthy patterns. For you to be a part of a high-value relationship, you must invest into the wealth that the relationship produces.

When you invest in emotionally nourishing connections, your inner world becomes more resilient and supported. From then, people are able to determine the capacity they can show up for you.

Investing into high-value relationships looks like becoming better at communication, advocacy when needed, or even practicing boundary keeping. Nevertheless, it all starts with you being able to do for yourself.

Emotional poverty is what keeps you stuck in survival mode, constantly reacting instead of intentionally living. When our emotions are poor, we are not able to focus on anything else except reaching some state of emotional satisfaction. Emotional poverty often leads to burnout, unfulfilling relationships, or overachievement driven by anxiety and fear rather than passion and truth. Ultimately, staying in emotional poverty, you end up wasting time that could be used to support you rather than harm you. It is easy to stay in emotional poverty when everything around you communicates that lack is the way things are supposed to be. You must create an environment around you that produces emotional wealth.

Furthermore, poverty is not synonymous with or a characteristic of being humble or honorable. You do not have to be poor or deny abundance in order to be considered modest. You can live in abundance and still be humble and honorable without falling to a corrupt nature.

In our emotional wealth, struggling and fighting to survive does not make us humble or modest. Believing that you must struggle to win is a poverty mindset, sustained by untrue beliefs. Emotional wealth is recognizing your ability to conquer and overcome, regardless of the circumstance you are presented with.

From a state of poverty, building emotional wealth must start with small, consistent practices that strengthen your emotional presence. Physically practice telling yourself what you like; talk to yourself out loud about your desires; express openly to yourself what you are scared of. If you are not able to be open and honest with yourself, you cannot build emotional wealth.

Some people have built an identity around appearing emotionally strong by constantly questioning or analyzing the emotions of others. On the surface, it can look like concern or emotional insight. In reality, those who show an excessive interest in other people's emotional state often struggle to maintain emotional control in their own lives. Focusing on others becomes a way to avoid confronting their own unresolved feelings.

If you do not openly acknowledge and express your emotions to yourself, no one else can support you. No relationship, friend, partner, or external source has the capacity to help in an area you have not admitted needs attention. Emotional growth begins with honesty. Until you make your inner needs known to yourself, then to the people you trust, healing and support cannot take place.

True emotional wealth is built on self-awareness, vulnerability, and the willingness to face your own emotional reality. In so doing, increase your emotional wealth by consistently self-checking, pausing, and self-honoring. Practice these areas so that you may gradually reshape your inner landscape and sustain the financial abundance that is guaranteed to you from aligning your emotional response.

Be honest with yourself *first,* then with others you trust about the past emotional trauma and wounds you have faced. Unresolved trauma very quietly drains your energy and impacts your clarity. No, do not trust everyone with your story. Do not share your story with social media if you have not done the work to heal from it. Do not share your trauma with strangers or new people you connect with. Sharing your story with people opens up an avenue for them to react and respond to it. Be intentional about who you release any part of your story to, even the wins, because, unintentionally, people can mistreat your emotional vulnerability.

In the need to share your story and express your trauma in order to move forward, write the story in a documented place only you have access to. From there, find a trained professional to help process what you have declared as truth.

Emotionally wealthy people navigate challenges with clarity. They are able to make decisions that are grounded. In so, their relationships are healthier, their boundaries are more clear, and their internal stability shapes how they lead and love. Emotionally wealthy people are successful because of their transparency and honesty. It is okay for everything not to be fine. It is okay to need support. It is okay to need time to accept reality with honesty and resilience. True emotional wealth includes accepting and communicating the full spectrum of our human feelings, including grief, anger, vulnerability, joy, and more.

Financial Wealth

Financial wealth is a principle designed by God. Wealth is not accidental or demonic. Financial wealth is a God-designed and God-given source. God designed wealth not for us to work toward; however, he designed wealth without already belonging to us. In so, we must claim our wealth and abundance as it is designed for us to achieve.

To be clear, financial wealth is money. And not just money, but an abundance of money and strategy in the relationship you express with money. This includes how to obtain it, multiply it, spend it, invest it, and use it.

Financial wealth is not a complicated definition. Financial wealth is not detailed. Financial wealth is not gathering just enough to survive to our next moment of lack. Financial wealth is the freedom to live and sustain your life without the pressure of being controlled by financial restraint.

Wealth overall is not the value we receive from being spiritually, emotionally, and financially aligned. Wealth is the byproduct of the reward we receive. The true reward we receive from intentionally aligning our spirit, emotions, and finances is value. Value is what produces wealth in every area. If you are more valuable, then naturally, more wealth will come your way. If you are less valuable, then wealth is not attracted to you. The value in anything shows you how to grow, multiply, create, and sustain.

Just like spiritual and emotional wealth, the value of your financial wealth begins with a self-awareness of your current state. From then, you must be able to learn how to communicate where you need healing and growth. From there, you can begin to apply strategies that allow you to practice skills that promote financial wealth. In so, when financial increase becomes evident in your life, you have the skills to steward it with purpose.

Many people desire financial wealth but disregard the journey of obtaining value. In so, they obtain more money, but lose it and have no strategies to rebuild it, because they have not encountered divine experiences that provided them with awareness and instruction.

You can not desire wealth but fear the characteristics wealth produces. Wealth produces responsibility when you possess it. Additionally, wealth produces a need for prosperity in every area of your life. You cannot pursue financial wealth and thrive in poverty-minded behavior at the same time. If you are operating at a high level of financial wealth, your poverty-minded behaviors cause you to disregard your wealth authority to create comfort in your poverty environment. In other words, when you increase financially, you must increase in every other area of your life. So, no, do not live beyond your means; however, everything you do must communicate and reinforce that spiritual, emotional, and financial wealth is a part of your identity.

Last, your financial wealth ensures that what you create on Earth is able to sustain throughout generations beyond your existence. The money you make while you are living should be able to care for and support your children, children's children, and children's children's children. Because wealth is a byproduct of value, that means your value must outlive your lifespan. In so, you must create some form of communication that connects your value to generations after you. Wealth overall is not measured by what you accumulate but by what you leave behind. Whether through storytelling, books, videography, sound, or written documentation, the value of your wealth is having the work of your spiritual, emotional, and financial alignment be accessible and true to the generations after you.

Chapter One C: The Reason You Keep Failing

Too often, we shy away from darkness. We shy away from darkness because we don't want to feel the pain of it. And as believers, we somehow have this ideology that we are supposed to be absent from pain if we believe in God. Well, that is wrong. As a matter of fact, the more you fully believe and trust in God, we have an unfair advantage in our pain being necessary for our development and growth.

Genesis 1:2, "And the earth was without form, and void; and darkness was upon the face of the deep. And the Spirit of God moved upon the face of the waters."

Before there was light, there was darkness. The darkness is what gives the light necessity.

We must be aware that it is dangerous to speed through scriptures. Nothing that is written and how it is written or translated is by mistake or happenstance. All writing is intentional and made true based on belief. But a lot of times, people speed through scriptures because we grew up thinking that if I get through it fast, then I must be proficient. Memorizing a quantity of scriptures and Bible text does appease God more than understanding scripture and Bible meaning.

For others, we grew up thinking and were taught that if you have to read it, then re-read or read it again, then there must be something wrong with us or our cognitive ability. We were taught that we should be able to read, comprehend, and reflect on a scripture once we speak it for the first time. That is an untruth.

When it comes to the Bible or anything that you read, there is nothing wrong with you reading and re-reading it. Additionally, it is encouraged that you read it again, then read it again with a highlighter, then read it again with a color pencil, because Bible text is complex and not our modern-day language. So, we must be intentional about decoding the language being used, then develop an understanding of what was written.

Because all writing is intentional, the Bible outlines the simple principles of God in a complex way. However, there are many places where the message and intent are made very clear once we understand how the author has written the text.

Even in needing to translate and decode Bible text, in the wisdom of what is written, you will find something new every single time that you read and come across it. God knows that the Bible has a lot of information in it. For myself, I would be pretty terrified if there was a book I should live my life by and it was only 12 pages. God allowed the design of the Bible to reflect a principle of human life. Although it is seemingly complicated, the principles within it are simple and achievable. This is why the Bible has been taught for years, and thousands beyond thousands of relevant messages have been taught from it week to week across nations. We receive the simple principles of God in different ways.

In its intentional order, after Genesis 1 verse 1 comes Genesis 1 verse 2. It is easy to skip over verse 2 because we want to get to verse 3, where God said, "Let there be light: and there was light." However, we miss what happened in verse 2 if we choose not to acknowledge what happens before light comes.

In Genesis 1 verse 2, "And the earth was without form, and void; and darkness was upon the face of the deep. And the Spirit of God moved upon the face of the waters." The Spirit of God was moving in the darkness before the light was even present.

If you are questioning the reason you keep failing, it is because you keep trying to skip past the darkness in your life. As a believer, you must prepare yourself for darkness because your time of darkness allows light to be relevant.

In order for a seed to grow, it has to experience darkness. It has to push through uncomfortable things in order to become stronger. Darkness is necessary.

As believers, the unfair advantage we have is our darkness being evidence of our success. Our pain is evidence of our success. Our belief that the situation we are in is evidence of it already being over. The way that we believe is our reward. Some people say, "Well, I don't have to believe in God to be successful, I just need to believe that success is possible for me." Guess what? They are right. Believing that success is possible for you is the principle. And principles work no matter how they are applied. But here's the difference between believing in God and believing in just yourself. When you are at a point of needing to give your darkness reason, you have no one and nothing to rely on for explanation. As a non-believer in God, your darkness serves no purpose. As a believer in God, when at a point of needing to give your darkness reason, you have a whole book, leaders, teams, and resources that support you in figuring out an explanation for what you are dealing with.

But, for some, going through darkness is not what keeps you stuck. You are willing to go through darkness to reach a reward. For some, the reason you keep failing is that when it comes to giving your darkness reason, you overcomplicate what is simple.

God's principles are simple. It is we, as humans living in great and advanced societies, who overcomplicate life and make our challenges seem more intricate than they truly are. The fundamentals are simple. If you want to be healthier, eat better, and move your body. Simple. Yet we overcomplicate it by saying, "My doctor said… I have pain in my… I can't… My medication… It costs too much…"

If you want to be smarter, read more. Simple. But again, we overcomplicate it with excuses like, "My eyes are bad… Reading makes me sleepy… I can't find a good book… Books are too expensive…"

All these complications, reasons, and justifications are nothing more than excuses wrapped in fear and doubt. We allow doubt to stop us faster than any real obstacle ever could. We allow it to talk us out of what we said we wanted to accomplish, even though the path forward is far simpler than we pretend it is.

The reason you keep failing is that you won't allow your darkness, your pain, your life experiences, whatever it may be that you declared was negative, we won't allow those things to be used for us to gain the wisdom necessary to sustain and be a good steward of what God wants to bless us with in the light.

We spend too much time focusing on what the darkness is and how the darkness hurt us, rather than focusing on why the darkness was necessary for us to get what we said we wanted.

Very quickly, we allow the doubt and limited mindset of people, ourselves, and everything except for God to become our God in explaining darkness to us. The reason we can never move forward is because we keep giving dominion to things God has already designed for us to have dominion over.

Some people may say, "Well. I got everything I ever wanted, and I didn't have to go through any pain or darkness to get where I am." That reason is, You Are Not A Threat. If your purpose is not challenged, then it is more than likely that your purpose is not valuable.

People fail because of a lack of clarity. People fail because they do not truly know what they want. When you lack clarity, you live in a constant state of hesitation, never fully committing to anything because your direction is unclear. Without clarity, you cannot commit, and without commitment, you cannot grow beyond your current level. Vague goals always produce vague actions, and vague actions lead to vague results that feel like failure. You must align your spirit, emotions, and finances to make beneficial decisions about where you are going. Your spiritual, emotional, and financial behavior must signify that the decisions you make are a representation of the wealth you desire. Indecision becomes the enemy of progress, creating a pattern of inconsistency that blocks all forward movement. Everything that you do must communicate that wealth is your status. You cannot be afraid to receive, use, and enjoy wealth if you desire it.

Fear, doubt, and guilt interrupt intentions long before you take meaningful action. Fear, doubt, and guilt create invisible barriers that talk you out of your own progress. When you overreact to discomfort and under-respond to responsibility, your emotions begin to control your outcomes instead of supporting them. Furthermore, your emotions signify to your brain that it must find comfort in what you are allowing to happen.

When we cry, it is an emotional response to feeling stressed, overwhelmed, or some level of vulnerability. It is our body's natural way to outwardly communicate our inner state of being. You cannot receive or desire wealth if your emotions are not set to handle the pressure of the wealth that comes. True wealth has no limit, so you have to be prepared to receive wealth at a high rate. And, you must be prepared to manage your desires with the wealth that you receive.

The reason people fail is because they use the financial wealth that they gain to satisfy the desires of emotional instability. This puts our financial wealth at risk because, just like crying, we do not control the ability to stop once it starts. If your emotions are unstable, once you begin to spend money to satisfy your desires, you are now a slave to your emotional desires without the control to stop. However, the way we move forward from this is by building a self-awareness of our emotional failings.

The reason you keep failing is because you haven't done the work to develop a self-awareness about what is missing from your value. In so, you find a need to serve your emotions and feelings over logic according to God's principles, because you fear outcomes not in your favor. Emotional instability makes effort unpredictable and inconsistent, which guarantees that results will be the same. In order to increase your effort in actively moving from emotional instability to awareness, be honest about the outcomes you have produced. Build a self-awareness about what has caused you to fail.

You do not control outcomes. You control your input that determines the outcomes. Therefore, you must practice the attributes of discipline. However, the reason you keep failing is because you won't allow yourself to stay in the discomfort of discipline. After all, your current mindset values safety over growth. In order to beat the cycle of failing, you have to be willing to be uncomfortable.

Our brains are designed to seek safety and security before anything. However, if you do not train your brain to make decisions that are uncomfortable in order to grow, you never develop the discipline needed to excel. Your brain physically strengthens every time you push yourself to do the difficult things you would not normally avoid. Discipline does not come from motivation, because motivation is temporary and unpredictable. If motivation were the ultimate catalyst in being the reason we achieve wealth, most people would have it. But in fact, motivation does not last, which is why the things most people want, they never get. We lose motivation daily due to us not being able to see or imagine results. However, discipline develops through repeated effort in the face of resistance, regardless of the result. Consistently choosing the uncomfortable actions that stretch us is what causes the result to come. If you desire wealth in any area, you have to continue building and stretching when you're motivated and when you're not.

Discipline is uncomfortable, which is why many choose convenience over commitment. Success is cumulative: it grows little by little through repeated effort. On the other hand, failure accumulates through repeated avoidance. The more we repeat anything we become more comfortable with it. Comfort weakens willpower in the brain.

Being comfortable allows us to stay safe and keep our minds focused on maintaining safety as long as we can. However, comfortability keeps us stuck. Being stuck can feel good because of its false sense of stability. This is why we feel comfortable relying on systems to support our financial income. It is not that we do not have the ability to create income personally; however, specific systems such as government-funded programs, living assistance, state-funded grants, and so on help to support a mask of stability. Yes, use money and services that are available to you for your benefit. However, if you are reliant upon a system to work in order for you to have stability and comfort, the safety you have built in believing that system will always work in your favor is false.

The reason you keep failing is because you rely on the input of systems that are out of your control for security and well-being. Now, this is not a bash to those who utilize government funding, state funding, or local resources; however, I am saying do not become fully dependent upon them in order for you to survive or have security. While it feels good to receive money and resources you did not work for, your stability is put at risk if a law changes, funding is denied, or you no longer qualify. It is unfair to you to stay stuck, reliant on systems that can affect your stability without notice or explanation. To go from poverty to wealth, we must learn to use government funding, state funding, or local resources as a tool to support our long-term safety rather than satisfying our short-term needs.

While it may feel good to stay comfortable, we risk the ability to have long-term security by finding comfort in short-term safety. We must embrace challenges because it increases our mental resilience and expands our capacity to grow. Practicing discipline in every area of our life reinforces our brain that it is allowed to make decisions that are of risk in order to promote growth. When we make decisions that support our growth, we have to take a step out of short-term safety.

The first time you speak up for yourself to an authoritative figure it can feel scary. You may not have been sure of the response you would receive or what the outcome would be. However, you speaking up was necessary for your point to be heard and you to practice having a voice. For you to grow in that moment required a step out of the short-term safety of possibilities negatively impacting you. To overcome the cycle of failing, you must be able to step out of comfort and take risks to support where you are going instead of where you are.

As it relates to wealth, this principle becomes even more important. Financial success requires long-term thinking, consistent action, delayed gratification, and the courage to face discomfort instead of escaping it. You have to command discipline in all of your behavior in order to reinforce discipline that promotes long-term growth. In your money, that looks like saving when you'd rather spend, investing when fear tells you to hold back, and learning new financial strategies to help you multiply your income when it feels inconvenient. All of these actions strengthen the same willpower muscle that builds emotional and mental endurance.

Wealth does not belong to the most talented; it belongs to the most disciplined. When you train your brain to lean into challenge rather than retreat to comfort, you develop the resilience required to build, manage, and multiply financial abundance.

Last, the reason you keep failing is due to the environment around you. You cannot control where you grew up or the neighborhood that brought you to where you are now; however, you have the ability to determine if what raised you is going to define you. You have a right and the power to discipline yourself away from normality in order to grow. In so doing, sometimes you will have to make a necessary separation from those who allow you to be the same. Separate yourself from people and environments that encourage and reinforce you to stay where you are comfortable.

Your environment shapes your behavior more than your desire does, because you adapt to the atmosphere you consistently sit in. You cannot grow in soil that does not support your seed, no matter how much talent or ambition you have. So, you must create an environment around you that supports your growth in every area of your life, regardless of making you feel comfortable while doing it. And at times, allowing this environment to be revealed requires a period of isolation for us to be able to receive the support when it is revealed.

You do not have to fail. You are not destined to have less or just enough. God has called you and demanded abundance in your life. So, if you are going to claim the abundance that is already yours, you must break the cycle of failing by choosing awareness of what got you to where you are. From then, move forward by doing the work in your spiritual, emotional, and financial decision-making to heal and excel.

PART II: REFRAMING YOUR MINDSET

Why Is This Part Needed?

AN OVERVIEW

This part ushers the reader into the divinely mandated seasons of obscurity, the moments when God intentionally pulls you away from visibility, certainty, and comfort. It reframes darkness not as punishment but as God's protective preparation, the sacred space where He matures what the world is not yet allowed to see. Here, we learn why God hides our calling until our character can carry it, why delayed clarity is an act of mercy, and why the absence of applause is often the greatest sign of divine favor.

This part exposes the emotional and psychological weight of obedience: why obedience often feels expensive, lonely, and profoundly misunderstood, and why the people closest to you cannot validate what they were never assigned to perceive. It examines the internal tension between the patterns of your old identity and the formation of your new one—the rupture required to birth transformation.

We will confront the reason God conceals the full plan, why He reveals direction only in pieces, and how He uses darkness to refine your voice, discipline your desires, and strengthen your spiritual muscles. This part dismantles the illusion that elevation begins in exposure; instead, it reveals that every season of influence begins in a season of hiddenness.

Ultimately, this section teaches that obscurity is not the delay of destiny; it is the development of destiny. God hides you to protect you, shape you, and ensure that when your voice emerges, it is rooted, sharpened, and ready to be received.

Chapter Two: Breaking Stagnation - How To Get Through Darkness

Popcorn generation, microwave generation, and so on. When change comes, we seemingly place the negative attributes to the younger generations; culturally, creating a divide between ages. Beyond the cultural age divide, society often fails to recognize that the imposition of change in societal norms is made visible by the active youth who are the voices of embracing innovation. In that embracing, it is our youth that are the catalyst for wide spreading cultural information amongst all of our generations in an attempt to bridge the gap between them and the wise. However, our youth hit a roadblock when faced with resistance to the new forms of innovation.

God intends for us to create innovation here on Earth. It is our purpose as people and our Biblical assignment to be creators. In a world today where people everywhere struggle with their identity, we often discredit the creator of us, by giving glory to the things that are not honorable to our purpose.

What is our purpose? Genesis 1:1 "In the beginning God created the heaven and the earth. To verse 26, "And God said, Let us make man in our image, after our likeness: and let them have dominion..."

You can not understand your purpose if you do not understand the one who created you. God gives us the purpose for our lives in order of importance by introducing us to His identity first. His opening statement to us (man) is not about what He is able to do, it is about the work He already did and intends for us to take advantage of. God creates. And after He tells us what He has made, He then makes it known that male and female are made in His image. Therefore, our purpose on Earth is defined by God in His detailing of what He is able to do.

Being that we are made in His image, our assignment as it is in Heaven is to create and innovate what God has already made good. He desires for us to make his good work better. How do we know this to be true? If God has made us in our image, that means all that He did and declared in Genesis chapter 1, verses 1-25 and beyond, we have the power and purpose to create and do those things too.

Genesis 1 Verse 1 "In the beginning God created the heaven and the earth." According to verse 1, we have the power to create entities bigger than ourselves that are greater than we can ever imagine. Such, those entities that we create produce wealth and prosperity more than what we can control.

Genesis 1 Verse 2 "And the earth was without form, and void; and darkness was upon the face of the deep. And the Spirit of God moved upon the face of the waters." We have the power and purpose to command the Spirit of God to move and activate things that are seemingly empty and dark. We have the power to turn nothingness into creation. Additionally, we have the power to proclaim authority and demand change in our life even when we can't see through the pain of the dark area we are in. We have the power to form, prepare, and plan for things that are bigger than us. If God took an Earth, without form and void, and made light from darkness, then we have the power to use our darkness to create light in our life.

Genesis 1 Verse 3 "And God said, Let there be light: and there was light." Light, as it is defined, is stimulation, illumination, consideration, or energy. According to verse 3, we have the power and purpose to call light to anything, regardless of its presumed difficulty or challenge. God commands light, and there was light. There is no middle passage between God commanding light and there being light. This means that there is no middle passage between us commanding anything to happen and the evidence of it already happening being present in our life. Once again, we are the evidence of what we desire being possible.

Furthermore, there is no challenge or difficulty prominent enough to even be mentioned in light coming forth, because anything that may present as an oppositional factor to God commanding light is not significant. Therefore, we have the power and purpose to do the same thing. Anything that is not significant to our light or desires, we have the power and purpose to disregard it.

Verse 4, And God saw the light, that it was good: and God divided the light from the darkness. We have the power and purpose to understand that darkness serves a purpose to our development. We have the power to make a clear distinction between the results of our discipline being beneficial against the process it took to achieve it. External sources would make us believe that the process of achieving our results was unnecessary or could have happened faster. When we are aligned with God, our process of darkness to light will only make sense to God *first,* then us, and no one else. Because we are believers, we have the power to determine that anything God has us experience, even if in darkness, is good for our light.

A plant needs light and darkness to survive. Like much of the Bible, each verse of Genesis 1 consecutively feeds into the next. The words of God are in perfect order, which means we must follow His outline for our life in order. Leading to the creation of God made in His own image, each word to the next is God giving us the details on what is necessary for us to flourish exceedingly in the next level of what He has prepared for us. In Genesis 1, God says after each creation that he saw it was good. This means that not only was God able to do the work, but the work he had done was strong and sustainable henceforth. While able to create without it, God was not satisfied until the works he had done were able to create and innovate more. This is why God made us in our image, because what we create is supposed to be able to innovate on its own once in the light.

In Genesis 1:12, Like the plant, grass, and herb yielding seed after his kind, and the tree yielding fruit, whose seed was in itself, after his kind, God saw that it was good. God's creation was more than good because He used the light, darkness, water, and beyond to help innovate what He desired to come from the Earth. Here, God is giving us an example of what innovation looks like. In darkness, we have the power to create without knowing what the final result is going to be. Like a seed, we must begin to invest into growing so that our roots are grounded in a foundation that is able to sustain once what we created in darkness comes to the light. So, even if we do not have the result, being in darkness is a signification that we must begin and start creating. God designed us to have dominion over every living thing on the Earth. So, as we create and innovate beyond what we claim to be dominion over, we must always remember that the significance of darkness is just as necessary as the light.

Darkness is what allows us to rest, cool, and grow in the face of God rather than in the judgment or knowing of people.

Matthew 7 encourages people to know men by their fruit. "A good tree cannot bring forth evil fruit, neither can a corrupt tree bring forth good fruit." As for a tree, plant, grass, and herb yielding seed, God allows the darkness to be offered as salvation for the fruit to come. What you produce is a testament of what you have gone through. No, you do not have to struggle in order to be successful; however, our experiences allow us the knowledge to ensure that what we learned from our season of darkness becomes our wisdom.

The roots of a seed are processed in darkness. God allows the seed a choice to grow. As the seed, a living thing, chooses to grow, it then has to go through a process of breaking through layers of dirt, soil, and, at times, manure, to benefit what is going to come forth in the light. Roots are the most important part of the plant's success. If the roots do not grow properly or strong enough, the plant will die and miss its fullest potential to shine and grow stronger in the light.

A plant cannot grow in light alone. It needs soil, dirt, and darkness to thrive. As its roots push through the layers beneath the surface, they must navigate the obstacles embedded in the very environment that makes growth possible. Stones, compacted earth, tangled roots, and barriers that present as challenges become the forces that strengthen the plant. In darkness is where a plant is nourished, its roots are shaped, and its life learns how to be sustained by water, nature, and time. All of this unseen work happens before God ever brings the plant into the light. Only then does the world witness what was being formed in the dark. The same goes for our life.

Genesis 1 Verse 5 "And God called the light Day, and the darkness he called Night. And the evening and the morning were the first day." In the image of God, we are a reflection of him. In so, according to verse 5, we have the power and purpose to name what surrounds us. God gave Adam the responsibility to name all of the animals. If we consider all of the different types of animals that are here on the Earth, it could be imagined that Adam became tired, frustrated, and just irritated by the weight of his assignment. Culturally, it is said that "God doesn't give more than you can bear." **THAT IS A LIE.** The scripture being referenced and highly misunderstood is 1 Corinthians 10:13. It is important to read the Bible for yourself and gain an understanding in your walk with God. You do not want to experience unnecessary darkness because of misguidance and lack of personal revelation.

For the older generations or what the Bible describes as 'the wise', we must not forget that our way of order and innovation was once *the new* before.

Some of us create and innovate in our life, then decide that we have reached a peak, because of our success or age. Adam was young when he named all of the animals. Noah was nearly 500 years old when he began building the Ark. Abraham was 75 years old when he was called to be the father of nations. Jesus was a boy when he had the assignment of performing some of His first miracles. Your age and current level of success do not define whether you must be ready for more growth. Your mindset is what prepares you for growth and further innovation. Achieving life's goals does not peak at retiring at the age of 65 or any specific number. In fact, the Bible mentions nothing about retiring and stopping what God has instructed you to create. You must continue your journey of creating and innovating your entire life. If God told us to create and innovate, when did He instruct us to stop? He doesn't. In our entire life and existence on Earth, we must create.

Some of you refuse to share your wisdom because you fear that what you have to offer is not relevant. And the truth is, it most likely is not. This means you have more to learn and must remain in your studious stature.

God identifies no age at which you are supposed to stop learning or creating. There is no such thing as "old and stuck in their ways." If you are stuck, you are making a daily conscious decision to stay stuck. You are reinforcing the lack of change in your daily behavior. Most likely, if you are stuck in one area that you refuse to change, you are probably stuck in multiple areas that need to change. Stop giving people advice based on your trauma and bad experiences if you have not healed from that moment. You must do the work to heal before you can share the wisdom you gained from your life experiences with someone else. As we gain wisdom, we are supposed to share and pour into the lives of others. However, the wisdom we share should come from what we've actually overcome, what we consistently practice, and what we're growing toward. There is no limit to abundance, so we must constantly be reaching for the maximum potential in it.

Now, do not feel like you have wasted time if you have just become aware of your responsibility to create and innovate throughout your entire life. It is time for you to reclaim the time that has been lost. Through God's grace and instruction, you will end up at the designated place you were to achieve through supernatural acceleration due to your obedience.

God will not blame you for embracing innovation and being wise in how you reclaim your time to create space for being obedient to His word and will; however, conviction and judgment will come upon you if the time you create from embracing God sent innovation is used to create space for you to go out of God's sight and do things that do not please Him.

One of the greatest challenges I faced was following God's instruction to go, sit, and wait. Many days, God instructed me to drive until I ran out of gas in my car. I am not encouraging you to do that; however, this was a test of my faith and obedience to God. I would go, sit, and wait for hours at a time. God told me that people or a person would come and drop cash money in my lap. So, I would sit with the windows open, turning my head around every few seconds to see if someone was going to show their face. I wanted to be obedient to God. I didn't want to miss the moment or question what He spoke to me. I found this stressful, because at this moment in my life, I was at complete zero. I had no money, using quarters to buy gas, using apps to find free food, depositing checks to go from negative to less negative in my bank accounts, driving in neutral, going down hill to save gas, asking people for money just to survive for a day. Instructing me to sit at gas stations for hours and pray for people's safety, yet not even having enough to put gas in my car to get home. Many nights and days, I floated on an empty tank, hoping and praying that my car would not cut off. God was testing my faith. God wanted me to prove that I could rely on him. Even in these times, there was never a day when I didn't make it home. In my season of darkness, I learned to rely on God to help me overcome obstacles. Ultimately, this made me stronger in the process, and in all, I learned a very simple principle:

Trust God's Timing.

Experiencing the lowest season of my life, going from a six-figure salary, stable job, successful romantic and platonic relationships, to a negative balance in all bank accounts, living with my parents, having my sports car repossessed, and complete isolation, God made me preach, and to everyone I spoke to, His message was to trust His timing. At my weakest point, I had to encourage others to be strong. This is how God works.

Because we live in a corrupt world, where many are lost, we must go through a process of stripping our ideas of comfort, success, Faith, and growth in order for God to build us back up the right way. The only way we can innovate what God has given us to its maximum potential is by correcting the idea we have about its existence, then using truth to push forward. If we are going to innovate, we must remove ourselves and others, so that we can hear the voice of God and be obedient to the process of Him reframing us.

Your Obedience to God's timing and voice is tailored to you and understood by you and you only. This shows how God loves us even more deeply to have an individual relationship with all of us. He does not minimize or group us together when it comes to the things that we need.

In my season of darkness, I kept asking God to speak for me. I wanted Him to explain my process to the people around me because I couldn't find the words myself. I battled with the tension between being obedient to God and being obedient to people. I knew that moving into my next season required following God's direction, yet part of me still wanted to satisfy everyone around me while doing it. I wanted to make everyone happy. I wanted everyone to understand the reasons behind my decisions.

I prayed that God would raise the spiritual clarity of those around me so they could see what I saw and understand what I was walking through. But the truth was that they were not meant to understand that season, and I was not meant to be validated in it.

From the outside, my obedience to God made me look untrustworthy, selfish, or even dishonest. It required me to remove people from the center of my decision-making, and that shift felt painful and disorienting. In my isolation, I wondered if the people I loved would ever accept me again after I stopped pleasing them and started obeying God. I questioned how I would explain myself, how I would rebuild trust, and how I would move forward after disappointing the very people I cared about.

What I did not realize then is that obedience to God does not always look responsible or reasonable in the moment. It often looks like disruption. It often looks like stepping away. It often looks like breaking patterns that everyone else is comfortable with. But God uses those seasons to pull you into creativity, innovation, and responsibility. He trusts you to create with Him, not to stay trapped in who others expect you to be.

Your season of darkness and isolation is not punishment. It is preparation. God teaches you how to have the authority, power, and responsibility to build the life He designed for us. To create. To innovate. To move in ways that do not need public approval. And sometimes the people you love cannot understand until they see the results of the work God told you to do in private. Hearing from God is the foundation of creating anything with God's guidance instead of everyone else's expectations.

I realized that at times I was trying to act as God. In the past, I had learned to temporarily let people, things, habits, and places go in obedience to Him, even when I didn't fully understand His plan. But I had never faced a situation where I had to release everything entirely into God's hands. Before fully being obedient to God's plan, I could never reach my fullest potential because I wanted to control my own outcome.

Learning to be fully obedient to God broke me. I felt shattered in ways I didn't know were possible. At my lowest point, I was fully exposed before God. In that brokenness, I began to understand His love for me more deeply.

God treats each of us like a designer original—carefully crafted, intentionally protected, and uniquely valuable. On the outside, in my past life, I may have appeared strong, capable, and in control. But God knew I could not move into my next season until I was transformed from the inside out.

He needed to change what people could see, what they would see, and what I had allowed them to see. Only then could I step forward with clarity, authenticity, and strength built on obedience, not on trying to please or control the narrative of my life.

This is the essence of embracing innovation. True creativity and the power to build come from learning to release control, trust the process, and take responsibility for creating in alignment with God's will. When you do this, you are free to innovate boldly, take risks confidently, and create something that lasts.

Chapter Three: The Perception Of Soon

Many times, we become frustrated with God because we believe, we have Faith, and yet we still don't see the outward result of what He promised. Sometimes we pray, claim scriptures, and act in Faith, yet the results feel delayed or invisible. We get frustrated because we explain to the people around us that the reason we are doing what we are doing is because of our obedience to God. Yet, we can't justify our actions because there are no Earthly results. We struggle with waiting for God's promises. Does this make God a liar? Does this make me false? Am I truly hearing from God, or am I just trying to make up a narrative that benefits my isolation? All of this creates tension in our minds, relationships, and obedience. If God is truly speaking to me, why is it not happening now? If God truly loves me, why is He embarrassing me publicly?

Our human minds can't reconcile what we see with what we believe. When we only see with our natural eyes, it appears as if everything we are doing is a waste of time. It is absolutely frustrating because it seems like we keep giving and pouring, but not seeing any results from what was promised. So, we begin to doubt, increase anxiety, and question God's plan. We start believing that what we are doing is not working.

As believers in Christ, we may even receive prophetic confirmation, yet we still wrestle with the timing of the results. And prophetic confirmation is not always a preacher or speaker with a mic being spooky over scary music.

Many times, prophetic confirmation happens in conversations, social media, videos, movies, etc. Nevertheless, we hear words that specifically confirm what God has shown us. However, we become further frustrated because our confirmation does not align with our reality. Yes, we hear from God clearly, but it is not the same as experiencing the full result. Learning to wait for God is the process He wants you to go through.

Just because God says it is going to happen soon does not mean it is going to happen now. We get disappointed, discouraged, and begin to doubt because how we imagined God's plan to work did not come to pass. God's ways are not our ways. His thoughts are not our thoughts. So, understanding God is understanding His perception of soon is different from our perception of soon.

Psalm 37 is about why the evil prosper and the righteous suffer. It gives us clarity about the tension between trusting God and waiting for His promises to show in our life. Believing that evil doers have more than those who are righteous and believe in Christ is false. Psalm 37 outlines the patience that we need to understand why God does what He does. When we are in God's perfect timing it allows us to sustain without the need to destroy.

Because of the corrupt world we live in, our desire is instant gratification. We want immediate results, because that's what we are conditioned to receive. When we want to find a new romantic partner, all we have to do is swipe and tap about 3 or 4 times to make a decision. When we want clothes, food, or just stuff that makes us happy, it only takes seconds to get it. When we have a question, concern, or need more information, we can have that problem solved immediately. While these innovations are beautiful in their ability to bring about immediate results with minimal effort, not all of them are of God.

There is no place in the Bible where God makes any person an immediate wealthy person. Nowhere in the Bible does God send someone a wife or husband within seconds. Nowhere in the Bible does God make someone a military leader or a King in a day. It does not happen because that is not how God operates. However, when we are conditioned to believe that everything we do must have an immediate result, it is easy to become discouraged. We get discouraged and slip back into things we know we should've left behind, just to get the immediate results. We go back to old jobs, people, habits, strategies, business models, and so on because they brought us results we were comfortable with, knowing how to create ourselves. However, when we insert our human impatience into our obedience, it affects God's perfect timing.

When you cook anything, you have to turn the heat down. Almost no recipe requires you to prepare the entire dish at maximum heat or temperature. If you try to prepare the entire dish at high temperature, something is going to burn. Yes, it may appear that the dish is complete; however, the fast time that it went through produces poor results. Even if the results are not poor, you miss the fullest flavor by rushing the process needed for the heat to cook the food evenly, without shocking it, causing negative effects. Simply put, *you gotta let it cook, Sweetie.* You have to follow the process of God to become well-rounded in the areas that need the most support for your journey. This means at times you will go through high fire. There are times when you need to be aggressive and ready to make strong moves. At other times, you need to be on low fire. Your consistency of the right things over an extended amount of time produces a better result with maximum potential. And when you follow God's plan in His timing, He will bring you out of the fire completely.

Our desire is instant gratification, but God's plan to build sustainable wealth requires spiritual, emotional, and financial preparation. God often works behind the scenes, shaping circumstances before the visible result occurs. What we do not realize is that going through the process, being frustrated, and having to trust God's way of survival is what makes us strong. God saying that something is going to happen "soon" is His time frame, not ours. However, because God loves us and cares about our total being, the process we go through aligns with our readiness and the fullness of what He intends. This is how He operates.

Often, our frustration comes not because God has lied, but because we have a very specific timeline in mind for how He should work. We have a tendency to set dates and plans for God's action in our lives. God gives us confirmation that something will happen, then we set a date in our minds for that to take place. We convince ourselves that God should act according to our calendar, our strategy, or our logic. What we fail to realize is that our expectations often come from experience, culture, or personal desires, rather than God's plan. We only expect things to happen based on the way we have experienced life in the past. In so, we become frustrated because the plan of how we saw it work in others is not working for us. God may say, He's going to open a door for a house. We become excited, pray, go to church, read our word, and fall deeply in love with God again while we are waiting. However, if we don't get that house within 1 year, we become discouraged and believe that the word may not have been true. For myself, I wanted to be married, because God had told me that I would. I became obsessed with making it happen instead of trusting God to take me through the process to become a good husband. Here's what I realized:

Sometimes we can not handle the confirmation, because it is a testament of us having to follow a process that is out of our control. I thought it would happen by this month or on this day. I expected God to open the door in a very specific way. However, I learned that I was limiting God to work only how I could imagine that He was able to do so.

When things we want from God do not happen, it feels like failure or delay. It feels like failure and delay because we prepare our hearts for the results and not the process to get there. Unintentionally, thoughts of doubt come upon us. We begin questioning God's faithfulness, our worthiness, or the validity of our prayers. And something I went through was going down a mental spiral of doubt, fear, and anxiety within seconds. It could be a moment's notice where I'm happy, feeling well, and one thought changes my entire mood because I allowed doubt, fear, and anxiety a place to stay. This is why it is essential to build a self-awareness of how you behave and think. The human mind often confuses "not yet" with "never." Because of the corrupt world that we live in, when things take an extended amount of time, we expect it to be untrue.

It is easy to prepare ourselves to have things, but we must learn to position ourselves to go through the process of being able to sustain them. Your response to God when He gives confirmation about what will happen in your life must gain clarity on how to prepare for what is next. Waiting on God is not failure or delay, but it is simply preparation. We must learn how to wait properly.

At the heart of our impatience is a natural desire to control outcomes and dictate how blessings should unfold. We desire for things to happen how we want them to happen. We can explore the human need for control beginning as newborns, toddlers, adolescents then adults. Children learn early to throw tantrums when they don't get what they want. As adults, we often retain this pattern when life doesn't go according to plan. We lash out, give up, display an outward expression of our frustration when things do not work how and when we want them to. This is a learned pattern from early human behavior. Our reaction to delayed outcomes reflects our struggle to trust someone or something greater than ourselves. It's a subtle form of idolizing control over God's timing. We become fixated and build an idol around *when* it happens, versus focusing on *how* God wants it to happen. In so, our desire for it to happen in our timing distorts the perception of God's timing.

We interpret waiting as failure, punishment, or a lack of care, rather than preparation. Misreading God's timing can create unnecessary stress and blind you from the work He has already done. Sometimes we are so frustrated with the process of waiting that we haven't realized God has taught us how to do things like pray consistently, consult Him with everything, minimize distractions, and so on.

In today's culture, waiting is seen as a burden, but in God's wealth, waiting is what builds maturity. We become impatient and fear being delayed.

You cannot be delayed if the only person who is supposed to receive what belongs to you is *you*.

While technology innovation has brought us convenience, instant gratification has conditioned us to expect immediate results in every area of life. In so, waiting triggers anxiety, fear, and the urge to rush, distract, or force outcomes. When things take too long, we assume that a problem has taken effect.

If we click a button and nothing happens, naturally, we may click again. If after the second or third click we see no type of change, we assume the button does not work. If we see some sort of change, but not the change we expected, we assume the entire system is out of order. This is how we treat God. We pray for something and get a little bit of confirmation. As we wait, we can see how something may work, but we don't see the results, so we become hesitant. We pray again, then God tells us to do the same thing, and we still don't get the results. So, we assume there must be a problem. We begin to blame ourselves, "Maybe I'm not hearing from God…" We begin to blame God, "Maybe God doesn't want me to have that…" From then on, we give up completely. We cannot see the results of anything if we don't allow the time for it to work. God is not a computer screen or application. He is God. So, when you activate your Faith and begin to wait, everything that you do will not produce immediate results; however, everything that you do will produce effective results.

The benefits of waiting are growth, clarity, and alignment. Waiting develops patience, discipline, and resilience. It allows our faith and creativity to mature while circumstances are aligning. When we wait and do so properly, the results we want are better. Rushing can actually prevent us from receiving the fullness of what God intends. Acting prematurely often leads to mistakes, missed lessons, or partial blessings. However, God's "soon" is perfect because it coordinates timing, people, and conditions for maximum impact.

Sometimes our waiting is not for us. At times, our waiting is to ensure the right people and systems are in place so that when we move forward, we are able to hit multiple targets at once rather than learning how to overcome each one as they appear. Nothing is more annoying than learning how to do a skill, then applying it, just to figure out you didn't learn how to do it the entire way; you only learned the first part. When you walk with God and follow His divine will, your obedience ensures completion and variety in how to achieve what you desire. God won't just show you one way to get something done. He'll reveal multiple paths and give you the strategy to learn how to do it at a level that can grow, stretch, and scale.

In so, we must redefine the perception of "soon." What God calls "soon" is often far different from what we expect. Understanding this difference is key to understanding our obedience. "Soon" is measured by God's purpose, readiness, and the alignment of circumstances, not human calendars. If we understand how God operates in things being "soon," we increase our capacity for more spiritual, emotional, and financial gain.

It is important to trust God's timing, even when it defies logic. God is God. He is not human or of human nature. In so, He does things that we don't understand, but it works in our favor.

Some may say, How are we made in our image, and there are things that God does that we do not understand? Because we are living, our life must become the example of God's truth. We are a reflection of Him. In so, what we do must make His word true. Patience and trust in God are evidence of Faith. Our consistent Faith is the evidence of God's word being true. When we learn to embrace "soon" correctly, we avoid stumbling under the weight of unpreparedness.

And the season of becoming prepared does not last forever. Your time will come. There are some people who fall in love with the process and preparation so much that they never walk into receiving the reward from it. Some people sabotage their process and stay in a cycle because they fear they will be lost when they receive the reward. People intentionally go backwards and disobey God, because they become comfortable being obedient and trusting God on the same level over and over and over. They mess things up, cause delay, say no, and quit so that they don't get too much from God at once.

If you are going to receive from God, you cannot be scared. God's blessings are overwhelming because he wants you to rely on Him for guidance with them. Therefore, he gives you a lot to depend on Him a lot. But it is not fair for you to stay in the same cycle of preparation and never move forward with walking into what God designed for you to have.

A basketball player can practice every day. They might attend camps, early morning workouts, off-season conditioning, work with private trainers, bio-medical engineering prep. All of this is useless if they never get to utilize their preparation off the court in an actual game. You cannot love the preparation so much that you don't stay consistent to finally operate in what you have prepared for. Ultimately, walking in what you have prepared for excels you further.

Alright, UncleBrandon, I get it. So, how do I practically change my perception of "soon?"

To embrace the perception of soon, we must align our hearts, minds, and actions with God's process instead of our own expectations. Acknowledge an awareness of where you allowed your perception of soon to override your obedience in God's divine timing. Ask God for forgiveness. From then, reflect on what God has already done. How has He sustained you? How has He kept you from being exposed? How has He revealed to you where you need growth? How has He shown you where you are going? Express gratitude for God's revelation thus far. Don't be afraid to write and record small victories and signs of progress to build confidence in His timing. Record videos, write in journals, make vision boards that only you have access to about where you are currently. You will be able to reflect on where you were once you achieve where you are going. From then, be intentional about your preparation during waiting periods. When God gives you an assignment, do not hesitate. Begin immediately. There is going to be a roadblock when you start. But keep your mind focused on your obedience producing reward, even if you do not understand why you are doing what you are doing. In all, keep your spirit grounded to avoid wasting energy on impatience, comparison, or anxiety.

Waiting is not a waste of time. Waiting is the foundation on which God builds miracles, blessings, and breakthroughs. God's "soon" is perfect, even when it doesn't match our perception. Accept that His timing is intentional and aligned with your preparation. Recognize that what feels like a delay is often a season of cultivation. And be encouraged to embrace waiting as preparation, not punishment. Shifting your perspective transforms your frustration into opportunity and growth. By trusting God's "soon," we position ourselves to receive blessings fully, without compromise or regret.

PART III: CONTROL

Releasing Control

AN OVERVIEW

This section uncovers our delusion that we can out-plan God — the same God who created Earth, time, and our environment while we lose our keys twice a week. Here we learn why surrender is the only real power move, and why every time we grab the wheel to our car of wealth, God just sighs like, *"Fine...crash,"* because we won't release control.

Chapter Four: How To Get Wealth The Right Way

It would be easy to name and justify a list of theories, paradigms, and behavioral practices that are rooted in the need for a human to have control. The desire to have or reclaim control can be justified and proven necessary as we dig deeper into the cultural implications for specific communities. Nevertheless, every human, regardless of background or belief, carries an innate desire to control their environment and their outcomes.

Control often feels necessary for survival and emotional balance. We desire control to stay safe. We desire control to be balanced in what we allow to come toward us. Being in control allows us to manage the narrative of our experiences. However, releasing control is non-negotiable if we are going to receive the maximum outcome of God's blessings.

Desiring control starts early in a human's life. It begins in childhood. Long before we can speak or reason, our flesh learns to crave control as a basic survival instinct.

As an infant, we are learning to trust or fear our environment. A baby relies completely on caregivers for comfort, nourishment, and protection. When those needs are met consistently, the child learns that the world is safe and that help will come when needed. But when needs are unmet, delayed, or unpredictable, the child begins forming the belief that they must always be alert, cautious, or self-protective. This is the birth of our control instinct: *If I cannot trust what is around me, I must take responsibility for my own survival.*

From then, babies become toddlers, where they begin to walk, explore, and express themselves. They test their environment to understand what they can and cannot control. Healthy boundaries and encouragement teach toddlers independence and confidence. But harsh criticism, strict environments, or inconsistent discipline create fear of failure, shame, and the belief that control is earned through perfection. This stage forms the internal message: *If I am not in control, I might get it wrong, and getting it wrong means I am not safe.*

As the child gets a little bit older, they begin making decisions, initiating activities, and taking creative steps. Supportive environments help them trust their instincts and take risks. But environments that punish mistakes or discourage exploration teach them that stepping out of line leads to disapproval. This reinforces a harmful belief: *I must control everything I do or I will disappoint someone.* Control becomes tied to identity and worth.

Then a child enters their school-age years. Naturally, they begin comparing themselves to others. They question their success compared to others around them. And if they are failing, their criticism makes them feel less than. This consistent need to compare drives an internal narrative: *I must control how others see me or I will appear inadequate.* From here, control becomes more about managing perception than managing behavior.

In early adolescent years, children struggle with defining their identity, values, and purpose. Being raised in environments that demand conformity or punish individuality and creativity, adolescents become confused and develop a fear of being misunderstood. To cope, they try to control their image, choices, and emotions to fit expectations or completely disobey the image expected of them. This embeds a new message in the child's brain: *If*

I don't control how I show up in the world, I might lose myself. If I lose myself, I won't be accepted.

All of this leads to adulthood. Early adults are tasked with defining the ability to form healthy relationships, depending on how comfortable they are with vulnerability. People who developed a strong sense of safety as children can share themselves authentically. Those who came from environments of instability or hurt often try to control their relationships to avoid pain. This is where many destructive patterns emerge: emotional withdrawal, over-attachment, manipulation, avoidance, or over-accommodation. The belief becomes: *If I don't control love, love will hurt me.*

Then, in mature adulthood, they seek meaning through work, creativity, and contribution. Mature adults believe that healthy development leads to confidence in one's ability to build and create. But people who have internalized fear and insecurity often over-control work, projects, or outcomes because productivity becomes tied to identity. The internal belief becomes: *If I don't control the outcome, I am not valuable.*

In older adulthood, later life, individuals reflect on their experiences and what they have built. Those who navigated their life stages with support and healing can release control and trust the process of life. Those who lived a life in fear and self-protection often cling to control tightly, attempting to prevent loss, disappointment, or regret. This final season shows clearly whether control has become a coping mechanism or a prison.

From our earliest moments to our final years, the human desire for control is shaped by how we experienced safety, autonomy, support, and identity. Control becomes our way of navigating the world when trust feels risky, when vulnerability feels dangerous, and when surrender feels impossible. This is why releasing control to God is not just a spiritual decision; it is an emotional and psychological reorientation. Releasing control to God requires unlearning the patterns we built for survival and embracing a trust that feels unfamiliar but freeing.

Our reaction to control often swings in one of two directions: 1) using it as power or 2) collapsing when we lose it.

1) On the first side, we use control as a way to maintain order, stability, or progress. Very naturally, our control becomes a tool for achieving desired outcomes. In so, it creates a sense of confidence, authority, and competence.

2) On the second side, when we lack control or fear we are in danger of losing it, we feel defeated, anxious, or powerless. We struggle because we can't maneuver life in the direction we want. And ultimately, loss of control triggers old wounds and trauma responses we have not healed from.

So, if our need for control goes unchecked, we will revert to the mental and physical behavior when we last believed that releasing our control was possible. For every stage of our life, we risk going back to as early as the infant stage, believing that *If I cannot trust what is around me, I must take responsibility for my own survival.* For some, this is the last mental place they were able to release control; however, their trust was mishandled, so they aged in number but never moved forward mentally.

Trauma doesn't just wound us emotionally; it rearranges how we see the world. When a person grows up in environments where safety, stability, or support were inconsistent, the mind learns to anticipate danger before it arrives. This creates a pattern where control becomes a shield for safety. We guard safety in believing that if we are in control, then we are able to prevent further harm.

Trauma conditions us to scan for threats, prepare for disappointment, or over-function to avoid chaos. Even when life has changed, the body and mind still respond as if the old danger is present. Because of this, many adults cling to control, not because they are stubborn alone, but because their nervous system is trained to believe that letting go is unsafe.

For some, control develops as a means of survival. People believe that if they can predict everything, then nothing can hurt them. In so, they develop narratives based on half-truths rather than full reality. For others, control becomes a way to manage relationships, emotions, or outcomes. Because their ability to not gauge harm was challenged, they learned to equate unpredictability with pain. Now, people who have these beliefs are not bad people. In fact, they do not make bad decisions. However, they have a false mindset that affects all of their behavior. The problem is not the desire for stability; it's the belief that control is the only way to stay protected in every area of their life. This is why surrendering to God feels so difficult.

Releasing control activates old fears of being unprotected or unseen. Trauma teaches us to depend on ourselves, but healing teaches us to trust Someone greater. And until we address the wounds that taught us to grip tightly, we will always struggle to release what God is asking us to place in His hands.

From childhood, our response to uncertainty, conflict, and unmet expectations affects our beliefs as an adult. Early wounds unaddressed don't disappear with age; they grow with us. Early wounds show up in our decisions, our relationships, and especially in our attempts to manage every detail of life. Unresolved trauma trains the nervous system to stay alert at all times. This is where hypervigilance forms.

Hypervigilance is the constant scanning, predicting, and preparing for something to go wrong. It produces fear of the unknown because unpredictability once brought pain. And over time, that same fear becomes distrust. Not just distrust of people, but a quiet distrust of God.

We say we trust Him, but our actions tell a different story. We try to micromanage outcomes because deep down, a wounded part of us believes: *If I don't control this, I'll be hurt again.* We become afraid to trust God because of being hurt by people. In so, we build an idol around our pain. Control, then, becomes more than a preference. It becomes a coping mechanism.

We numb anxiety, avoid vulnerability, and create the illusion of safety by maintaining control. When we can dictate what happens next, we feel temporarily protected. But this kind of control is fragile, because it is built on a half-truth. Control only works as long as everything goes according to our plan. In life, whether we are believers in Christ or not, things rarely go the way we want them to.

Sometimes control can look like strength from the outside. It is rooted in unresolved fear. Many people who seem confident, decisive, and "in charge" are actually managing old wounds that were never healed. Control becomes their armor, their shield, and their way of staying ahead of potential hurt. But real strength isn't found in gripping tightly. Real strength begins with healing, surrender, and trusting a God who is not bound by our trauma. From then, we can recognize that our ability to release control is actually stronger than a constant need to have it.

Trusting God fully and being in control do not work together. There is no in-between. You must follow His word or don't follow it at all. In the process of building wealth, you develop and feed a spiritual, emotional, and financial tension when you claim to trust God, but want control of what happens.

We often claim to trust God, right up until He asks us to release control.

Many people say they trust God, but the truth is they trust God with conditions attached. We trust God until His instructions make us feel comfortable. We trust God when the outcome seems predictable. We trust God when His plan aligns neatly with our preferences, our timing, and our understanding. But the moment God's direction disrupts our expectations, beliefs, or requires us to move without clarity, our trust becomes hesitant. We don't struggle with God's voice; we struggle with the parts of His voice that call us into the unknown.

This is where frustration begins. We want God to act in ways that make sense to us. We want Him to communicate like we communicate, to operate according to human logic, and to follow the emotional scripts we're used to. But God is not human. He does not respond out of fear, urgency, insecurity, or pressure like we do. We want His movement to be predictable and convenient, but His sovereignty is not built on our comfort.

When God does not act the way we expect, we feel confused or disappointed, not because He failed us, but because He refused to be controlled. We imagine that our diligence, our sacrifice, or our emotions should earn us the right to dictate how God moves. But God does not bend under the weight of our expectations. He does not speed up because we are impatient, or slow down because we are scared. He does not adjust His method to match our preferences, and He certainly does not modify His will to satisfy our need for clarity before obedience.

This is the tension we rarely admit. Our frustration with God in releasing control is a deeper frustration with not being God ourselves. We want the power, the foresight, the timing, and the authority that only God has. We want to control the process and the outcome. We want to decide the how, the when, and the who. And when God interrupts that desire, we interpret that disruption as disappointment.

However, the frustration is not about God. It's about the loss of the illusion that we were ever in control to begin with. Trust anywhere requires surrender, and surrender requires acknowledging that we cannot control the narrative. We cannot take God's place in our own story. The sooner we let go of trying to be our own God, the sooner we can experience the peace, guidance, and provision that only He can give. But it starts with renewing our mindset.

Before God blesses us, He must renew our mindset. The first step to renewing our minds is releasing control to Him as Father. It is impossible for a child to tell the father how to be the father. You cannot tell a parent how to raise you unless you have already raised yourself.

Control and surrender cannot exist in the same place. Control demands authority, while surrender demands releasing it. Control insists on directing the outcome while trusting the One who sees beyond the moment. Trying to control while claiming to surrender creates internal conflict. We create a spiritual, emotional, and financial tug-of-war between our desire for safety and God's desire for our growth. True surrender requires letting go of the illusion that our plans, timing, or understanding are superior to God's. As long as we cling to control, we leave no room for Him to operate on our behalf.

A child cannot tell the father how to be the father. A child may have preferences, desires, or fears, but it is the father who carries the wisdom, strength, and responsibility to lead. Likewise, we cannot dictate to God how He should guide us, bless us, defend us, or develop us. Yet we often approach Him with a posture that says, "Do it this way," or "Do it now," or "Do it exactly how I imagined." But a child trying to lead the father is a picture of confusion. It reverses the relationship and places pressure on the child that the child is never meant to bear.

Past traumas, unchecked, distort our relationship with God. When our early experiences taught us that authority figures were unreliable, inconsistent, or unsafe, we unconsciously transferred those wounds onto God. We start relating to Him through fear, self-protection, or hyper-independence. Instead, we must trust God's intentions and not brace ourselves for disappointment. We must rest in God's promises and not prepare for things to fall apart.

To heal from the need to have control requires a different posture in our life and relationship with God. Healing requires accepting God's power, sovereignty, and goodness as truth. Healing requires the acknowledgment that God is not like the people who hurt us, abandoned us, or failed us. His intentions are not tainted by human limitations. Surrender becomes possible when we recognize that releasing control is not weakness; it is wisdom. It is choosing to trust the One who sees the whole picture when we only see pieces.

When we release control our emotional stability returns. The anxiety of trying to manage every detail begins to dissolve. Our Faith expands because we finally give God the space to prove Himself. Clarity emerges because we are no longer clouded by fear and self-protection. This is the renewal of the mind, shifting from survival mode to surrendered trust in God. This is the only way we can fully walk in the freedom, creativity, and abundance that God designed for us.

If you're unsure whether unresolved trauma is driving your need for control, use the questions below for honest reflection. If you answer "yes" to any of them, it is time to begin the journey of healing and fully surrender to God.

Reflection Questions:

- Do you feel anxious or unsafe when you're not in control of a situation or relationship?
- Do you often assume things will go wrong unless you manage every detail yourself?
- Do you struggle to trust others with outcomes that matter to you?
- Do you feel responsible for protecting yourself, even when support is available?
- Do you become frustrated or fearful when God's timing doesn't match your expectations?
- Do you equate surrender with weakness, vulnerability, or loss of safety?
- Do you have difficulty resting, delegating, or letting go because you fear

being disappointed again?

If you hesitated or struggled accepting or acknowledging any of these questions, you owe yourself healing to move forward. Do not be the reason you don't get what you fully deserve because the truth about your trauma offended you. Heal from it and walk into the abundance God has designed for you to have. Surrendering to God's will and plan enlarges the capacity to receive spiritual, emotional, and financial wealth.

Just let go.

Releasing control is not weakness. We cannot heal, grow, or progress while trying to be our own God. The need for control is rooted in fear, but surrender is rooted in trust. Be encouraged to let go and allow God to be everything He promised. God will be your protector, provider, guide, and source if you let Him. You make your life harder when you try to do God's job, and you make it freer when you let Him do what only He can do.

PART IV: EVIDENCE THAT GOD WAS RIGHT

What Happens When Obedience Pays Off

AN OVERVIEW

This section reveals the seasons when obedience finally produced fruit — the breakthroughs, wins, confirmations, and victories God used to prove His hand was on our assignment all along. It walks us through our personal wins not as bragging rights, but as evidence of what becomes possible when we stay faithful, consistent, and aligned.

This section reveals how every win carried a lesson: how celebration taught stewardship, how progress taught humility, and how success required just as much character as suffering.

This part reminds us that celebrating wins is not vanity — it is spiritual memory. It is how we mark God's faithfulness, measure our growth, and keep us from returning to the mindset we prayed our way out of.

Chapter Five: Celebrating the Wins

Celebration is not a luxury in the life of a believer in Christ. Celebrating is a Biblical necessity and an act of faith, honor, and stewardship to God. Many people struggle to celebrate themselves because of guilt, fear, humility taken out of context, or a history of always being in survival mode. Celebration is not unspiritual or self-centered. It is a Biblical principle that reflects gratitude and acknowledges God as the source of every blessing. Celebrating wins is not just emotional. Celebrating is strategic and healthy for long-term vision, creativity, and wealth building.

King Solomon is one of my favorite blueprints for celebration in the Bible. Scripture makes it clear that celebration is not only permitted but it is commanded and modeled by God's chosen leaders.

In 1 Kings 8, Solomon dedicates the temple he spent years building for God. It was massive; some people died, many sweat, tears, and finances went into making it happen. At the dedication of the temple, God responds with a blessing. From then, a national celebration of God's blessing erupts.

Solomon's celebration was anything short of a casual gathering. Scripture describes a moment so extravagant, so overflowing, that it became one of the most remarkable celebrations in Israel's history. Food filled the streets, meats, grains, fruit, and wine were so abundant that no one who came left hungry. Families traveled from distant regions, and entire communities journeyed together just to be part of what God had done. What began as a dedication ceremony grew into an entire two-week festival of nonstop joy, music, dancing, and communal fellowship.

Imagine the sound of thousands of voices singing. Imagine the fragrance of meals being prepared across acres of land. Imagine the unity of a nation coming together, not in crisis, not in war, not in famine, but simply to celebrate the goodness of God. This wasn't quiet or conservative; it was public, expressive, and unrestrained. Solomon understood that when God does something monumental, the response should reflect the magnitude of the blessing. In other words, celebration is an expectation, not an option.

Many people today struggle with celebration because they equate it with arrogance, waste, or distraction. But Solomon shows the opposite.

When God blesses, He expects His people to honor Him by enjoying what He provides. God did not fill the Temple with His glory only for the people to shrug and go back to work. He designed that moment to be marked, remembered, and magnified through celebration.

This is why the feast mattered. It honored God by showing gratitude, not just with words but with joy. Celebration is a spiritual discipline. It acknowledges 1) *God kept His promise, 2) God made a way, and 3) God deserves the glory.* When you participate in the blessing God gave you, you are not being selfish; you are being obedient.

Solomon's celebration was both outward and inward. Publicly, it showed the surrounding nations that Israel served a God who fulfills His word. The joy of the people, the unity of the celebration, and the overflow of abundance all testified that God's hand was on them. Their celebration was a sermon without a pulpit.

Privately, the feast did something just as important. It reminded the people that obedience produces fruit. They had witnessed the long process, the labor, the sacrifices, the construction, the prayers, and now they stood in the harvest. The celebration reinforced that the journey was worth it. It taught them that God was not just a God of instructions and sacrifice, but He was a God of reward, joy, and fulfillment.

Celebration teaches us that when we obey God, we will see goodness. If we remain faithful, we will reap.

Celebration should be a form of outward stewardship and wealth-building, not a burden. True celebration does not drain you; it multiplies you.

Many people avoid celebrating their wins because they fear it will derail their progress, waste money, or create unnecessary attention. But Biblically, celebration is not an interruption to success; it is part of the process that sustains success. Celebration is a tool of stewardship. It honors God, honors your journey, strengthens your relationships, and keeps your creativity alive. When done correctly, celebration becomes a strategic investment into your future, not a financial setback.

Healthy celebration restores you emotionally. Long-term discipline without moments of joy leads to emotional fatigue. Celebration serves as a reset for your mind and spirit. When you allow yourself a moment of joy, your body comes out of survival mode and into creativity mode. This is why so many creatives, musicians, and entrepreneurs receive their best ideas while relaxing, traveling, or simply enjoying themselves. For example, countless hit songs, business concepts, and partnerships were birthed from casual celebrations or relaxed gatherings where no one was "working," yet ideas flowed freely.

Celebration strengthens your network. When you invite people into your wins with intentionality, you give others the opportunity to support you, collaborate with you, and connect with you. A celebration creates a shared memory and shared emotional investment. This is how professional and spiritual family bonds form. A small listening event in a home, a brunch with collaborators, or a virtual celebration with supporters can shift your relationships in ways that purely "professional" conversations never could. Celebration builds relational wealth, which is often more powerful than financial wealth.

Celebration also honors the work you put in. When you recognize your own effort, discipline, and resilience, you reinforce your identity and confidence. You remind yourself that what you carry is valuable and that what you produce has meaning. This is especially important for creatives who often work long periods without applause. A musician hosting a release concert, an author hosting a signing event, or an entrepreneur honoring the anniversary of their business is not just celebrating an outcome; they are strengthening their belief in their own gift.

Intentional celebration can also create income opportunities. Many celebrations become platforms for new revenue, brand exposure, or partnerships. Here are more examples that illustrate how celebration can multiply wealth:

For musicians:

- Hosting a release party where guests buy merch, tickets, or exclusive editions of your music.
- Turning live performances into content that attracts sponsorships.
- Selling behind-the-scenes access to the process of your album creation.

For creatives:

- Launching a new project during a celebratory event to maximize attention and support.
- Offering limited-edition artwork, signature items, or print runs connected to the celebration.

For entrepreneurs:

- Hosting a customer appreciation event that doubles as a preview of your next product.
- Using celebrations to announce collaborations with other brands.

For families:

- Turning life milestones into moments that build legacy by inviting extended family to share stories, wisdom, and support that strengthen generational connection.

For influencers or public figures:

- Using celebratory content to increase engagement, which leads to higher brand partnership rates.
- Offering webinars, workshops, or online events tied to the celebration themes.

Celebration is not just about joy; it is about momentum. The act of celebrating signals to your mind, your community, and the spiritual realm that you expect more good to come. Celebration literally conditions your mind to receive bigger blessings because it teaches the brain to associate achievement with joy rather than fear or guilt.

When celebration becomes part of your lifestyle, wealth flows more easily because you are no longer operating from scarcity. You begin to understand that success is not something you chase; it is something you steward. Celebration becomes the bridge between where you are and where God is taking you next. It keeps wealth circulating, creativity expanding, and relationships deepening. It keeps you emotionally whole enough to continue building, producing, and growing without burning out.

In God's order, stewardship is not only about saving or managing. It is about activating. Too often, we teach and understand stewardship as holding on to money. While that is included, stewardship is also knowing how to use that money to create further opportunity. Being a wealthy steward allows celebration to activate gratitude, multiply faith, expand influence, and replenish your emotional and spiritual energy. When you celebrate intentionally, you do not lose anything. When you celebrate, you gain clarity, confidence, community support, and new opportunities that lead directly to more income.

True celebration does not cost you. It compounds you. It multiplies the grace on your life, the joy in your home, and the wealth in your hands. Celebrating your wins is not a financial setback but a creative strategy that keeps wealth circulating. Do not limit yourself to believe that celebrating is not a principle of God. He desires for us to enjoy the abundance we create on Earth. Other people must see the outward expression of celebration in God's blessings.

God uses plants, trees, fruit, and overall harvesting as a way to communicate his process. All throughout the Bible, God references seasons, soil, roots, pruning, waiting, and reaping because He wants us to have a physical example of how He operates. Harvesting helps us to understand that blessings are supposed to feel like abundance and not anxiety. When God leads you through a process and brings you into a season of results, He does not expect you to shrink back or feel guilty about what you've gained. He expects you to taste it. To enjoy it. To honor the work He empowered you to do. Your success is not meant to sit in shadows. Your success is designed to encourage you, uplift you, and build your confidence in His ability to guide you.

And while celebration often looks like joy, laughter, or rest, it also functions as a powerful spiritual and emotional reset. Celebration gives you space to breathe, reflect, and receive clarity that you can't access when you're constantly working. Even while working toward the large outcomes, it is important to celebrate the small wins. Celebrating the small wins might look like taking a quiet day to yourself, hosting a small gathering with people who truly understand your journey, creating a moment of gratitude with a mentor, or taking time to enjoy and talk about something you created or learned. Whatever the form, celebration should leave you feeling renewed, grounded, and aligned with God's intention for your life.

Hiding your success dishonors God. Concealing your wins is not humility. Hiding your success is fear. We fear judgment. We fear opinions. We fear being misunderstood. But fear was never meant to be the lens through which you interpret blessing. If God has openly blessed you, there is no reason to respond in secrecy. People need to see what obedience looks like when it produces results. People need to see what Faith looks like when it finally materializes. Your life becomes a living testimony. Everyone will not have the spiritual maturity to study the Bible and look at plants as God's process. There are some people who will never pick up a Bible and read a verse about God-ordained abundance and wealth. However, for those people, they need to see wealth and abundance in you.

Celebration is not arrogance. Celebration is gratitude to God. You being able to openly acknowledge and display the abundance God has given you shows that your heart is postured correctly.

So, enjoy your fruit. Enjoy your harvest. Enjoy the moment God carved out specifically for you. Let your joy be evidence. Let your gratitude be visible. Let your life show that obedience actually leads to something real. And once the celebration quiets down, once the excitement settles and daily life calls your name again, you return with intention.

After celebrating, you are not to go back to the person you were before the breakthrough. The goal is to carry the joy, clarity, and perspective you gained from the celebration into your everyday rhythm. God didn't walk you through the process so you could abandon the growth once the party ended. Don't sabotage what you have built out of false humility, fear of judgment, or of further success. God intended for your celebration to anchor confidence so you could walk into your next with steadiness, gratitude, and renewed purpose.

And after you celebrate, you have to return to life without losing joy.

One of the most overlooked parts of Solomon's celebration is what happened after the two-week feasts and festival. In verse 66 of 1 Kings 8, the people went home "joyful and glad of heart."

This small detail in verse 66 carries a profound truth. The celebration ended, but the joy didn't. The music stopped, the crowds dispersed, and the feast concluded, yet the people returned to their tents, returned to their ordinary routines, everyday responsibilities, and familiar surroundings with a renewed posture. They went home carrying something the celebration had deposited in them: gratitude, emotional stability, and a fresh awareness of God's goodness. Their outward environment didn't change, but their internal mindset did.

Celebration is a moment, but joy is a discipline. Your celebration may last just a few days, but you must make a conscious decision to choose joy daily.

God never intended for His people to celebrate publicly and then return home privately discouraged, depleted, or doubtful. God wants what happens in your celebratory moments to reshape how you live once the moment is over. Celebration is supposed to alter the way you think, the way you work, the way you create, and the way you move through your daily life. It is meant to strengthen your emotional capacity, not just entertain your emotions. It is meant to anchor your belief, not just excite your feelings.

This is where many people struggle. We celebrate, the applause fades, the event concludes, the milestone passes, and suddenly, they don't know how to transition back into the rhythm of everyday life. We begin to slip back into old habits, insecurities, self-doubt, overthinking, or patterns of fear we thought were left behind. But the true test of spiritual, emotional, and financial maturity is not how loudly you celebrate; it is how steadily you live once the celebration ends.

So here is the challenge: When your moment of celebration is over, refuse to fall back into old thinking. Do not let familiar surroundings pull you into familiar mindsets. Move forward with intention. Carry your gratitude with you. Let the joy you gained from celebrating shape how you handle your responsibilities, how you manage your time, how you pursue your goals, and how you respond to challenges. Walk with confidence, not because life is perfect, but because you are no longer walking as the version of yourself who doubted, feared, or minimized what God has done.

The celebration may have been temporary, but the transformation it initiated is meant to be permanent.

Celebrating correctly resets your identity. It reminds you that you are not the struggling version of yourself you once were. It breaks the poverty mindset by teaching your heart that increase is not dangerous, unfamiliar, or temporary. It expands your gratitude, and gratitude expands your capacity to handle more. Celebration trains your mind to see success as something normal and sustainable, not something random that you stumbled into.

God's favor naturally flows through people who steward success well. God honors those who do not taint their blessing with fear, nor do they distort it with pride. They simply receive it, honor it, and grow from it.

This is where generational blessing begin. When you model a healthy relationship with success, the people watching you, your children, your family, your community, inherit confidence instead of scarcity. They begin to expect good things rather than fear them. Your legacy is shaped not only by the victories you achieve but by how you handle the fruit of your labor once it appears.

You must celebrate without feeling guilty. You were not created to shrink when you win; you were created to shine when God's goodness shows up in your life. Ultimately, understand that your victories are not accidents, and they are not burdens. Your victories are evidence that the process worked. They are proof that obedience matters. So celebrate boldly. Celebrate creatively. Celebrate publicly. Celebrate without apology. Your celebration honors God, strengthens your spirit, and lays the foundation for the next miracle you are being prepared to receive.

Some people still feel confused, heavy, or even depressed after a win. And that emotional shift deserves space, clarity, and understanding.

When you celebrate well and steward well, there is no guilt in success.

Chapter Five A: Feeling Confused After A Win

Sometimes there are strange emotions that follow success.

One of the hardest parts of winning is admitting that sometimes victory doesn't feel the way you imagined it would.

People assume that achievement automatically creates joy, instant fulfillment, and peace. Yet many people reach a major achievement only to find themselves overwhelmed by sadness, confusion, or emotional numbness. This happens not because they're ungrateful, but because winning disrupts the patterns they've lived in for so long.

Success replaces structure with space, and that space can sometimes feel foreign.

So, why is it that I don't feel the space until I actually achieved the goal?

The pursuit toward your outcome kept your mind focused. The struggle kept you alert. The pressure kept you driven. When the pressure lifts, you suddenly face a blank emotional landscape you never prepared for. It is natural to encounter emotional tension following major accomplishments. There is nothing wrong with you. You're not broken. You're transitioning.

Elevation comes with isolation. Before God elevates you, He must expose those who cannot go with you. Every win and moment of celebration reveals someone or something you've outgrown. Elevation clarifies relationships. Some people only knew how to love you when you were small, struggling, or predictable. They were comfortable when you needed them, leaned on them, or looked up to them. But success forces their unresolved insecurities to the surface. Suddenly, they become distant, critical, or passive-aggressive, not because you did anything wrong, but because your growth confronts their stagnation. This necessary separation is not punishment. It is protection. God removes voices that would mishandle the next version of you, sabotage your confidence, or pull you back into environments you prayed your way out of. Much of the confusion after a win is not about the achievement itself. Feeling confused after a win is the grieving process of your old life. You're mourning who you lost, who you outgrew, and who you can no longer be.

For others, people feel depressed after a win because the pursuit toward it felt safer than the achievement. Chasing a goal provides structure, adrenaline, and purpose. You always knew what to do next. You always had something to prove. You always had more to learn. When you finally win, that internal fire quiets. The brain and body, after months or years of striving, releases tension. However, we are not told that the release of tension can feel like emptiness. Your mind has to recalibrate into learning how to function without constant pressure.

People rarely talk about how uncomfortable it is to shift from "fighting for it" to "living in it." The discomfort does not mean the win wasn't real or deserved. It means your internal rhythm is adjusting to a new pace. Often, that new pace is one that is healthier, but unfamiliar.

After a win, doubt can enter your mind, and you lose clarity. Even though untrue and proven false, you would begin to believe that your success is luck, you're not ready, or you don't deserve it.

Do not allow a false insecurity to take reign in the exact moment you should be walking in confidence.

Your growth threatens cycles. Your breakthrough unlocks freedom for others. Your visibility invites influence. If you shrink, hide, or sabotage yourself right after God elevates you, it can make a ripple effect of the maximum potential of your calling before it begins. This is why not everyone should have access to you when you reach high accomplishments.

Success makes you visible, but visibility can become a liability when the wrong people have access to your vulnerable places. When people are close to you, your transition is often seen before your transformation is complete. People watch your journey without understanding your process. Some only know one chapter of your life and speak on it as if they read the whole book. This creates pressure to explain yourself, defend yourself, or hide yourself. But not everyone deserves access to the explanation of your growth. There is a difference between protecting your pain and protecting your peace. Protecting your pain leads to avoidance, irritability, and shutting down. Protecting your peace leads to boundaries, clarity, and emotional honesty. The confusion you feel after a win often comes from overexposure. You feel confused because you allowed too many opinions close to your process. Many times those opinions are from people who don't and will sometimes never understand.

So, how do I rebuild momentum when feeling emotionally dull after a win?

Here are simple, grounded steps to recalibrate your mind and spirit when success leaves you feeling off-balance:

1. Move from protecting your pain to protecting your peace.

Spend intentional time alone. Journal. Pray. Reflect. Let your emotions surface instead of stuffing them. Communicate with God about what you are feeling. Identify what feels uneasy or out of place.

2. Release control and maintain your blessing.

Celebrate the win, but also take time to understand it. Learn how to sustain and grow what God has placed in your hands. For example: Graduates can study their field more deeply. New homeowners can learn the basics of house maintenance. Newly promoted individuals can study leadership. Learn how to maximize where you are.

3. Accept that life is not linear.

Success does not create an effortless life. Confusion is not failure. Growth is not always comfortable. The path forward will include pivots, pauses, and moments of uncertainty. Develop a consistent awareness that this is normal.

Feeling confused after a win is not a sign of failure; it's a sign that your capacity is expanding. You are carrying more responsibility, more visibility, more opportunity, and more purpose than before. Your emotions are simply catching up to your reality. You are not going backward. You are not losing your spark. You are not crazy. You are adjusting to a new level of becoming. A new level of becoming requires a different version of you. This discomfort is not punishment; it is preparation.

You are not confused — you are evolving.

Chapter Six: Birth Of My Assignment

God uses seasons of drought not just to prove that He is God, but to help *us* see it for ourselves. My story is not simply about what I went through, but in sharing, I wanted to create a roadmap for you to understand why your season looks the way it does and how it's leading you toward spiritual, emotional, and financial wealth. Now, this is not a story of how I started in absolute poverty from an inner city community and became a multi-millionaire. However, this is the portion of my life when my perspective changed into learning how to build spiritual, emotional, and financial wealth. This was the turning point for where I am now.

Before the Drought: Comfort, Success, and Control

Straight out of graduate school at 22 years old, I was working with the military as a social worker, making money as a musician, and producing music on the side. I was ready to move out of my parent's house, live on my own, and enjoy the life I thought I deserved. Everything was lining up.

Then God interrupted my plans.

While in school, I built a solid reputation. I was respected in many university departments across the region, involved with audio tech crews, connected to instrumentalists around the city, and known by multiple teaching programs within different school districts. I graduated at the top of my class — degrees, awards, and endorsements behind my name. Every door seemed open.

But spiritual maturity teaches you that open doors don't always mean it's the door God wants you to go through. And before God trains your hands for abundance, He often strips away what you think is keeping you stable.

So, here I was. I had built something, earned something, expected something...and then life flipped.

Lesson #1: God will interrupt your comfort to protect your calling.

Having my master's degree at 22 years old, working an above entry-level government job, and spending money how I wanted to, I felt like I had made it. I knew the favor of God was on my life, but I gave myself a lot of credit instead of God. I gave myself credit for building the connections, receiving the endorsements, making the straight A's. I thought that even though God was in my life, it was me alone making those moves to put me in the position that I was. I felt like I had built my own reputation. I knew that I could get and do anything that I wanted simply because nobody was going to tell me no. I never expected a no, because anything I wanted, I got it. Anything I desired, I had it. Anything I went after, I received it. Every time people asked me how I always got selected, chosen, more money, the opportunity, and more, I always told them, "Because It's Me." And not too long would God allow Him not to get the glory for His works. So, God took what I was most proud of and stripped it away from me. Not my awards, money, or relationships. The first thing God challenged me with releasing control to Him was my identity.

Out of obedience to God, I quit my job and started working in music full time. Everything was okay. I had a good amount of money saved up where I could keep up my quality of life without suffering. Still refusing to give Him the full glory for helping me sustain, God sent me through an even deeper process to get my attention.

The gigs, shows, and music-producing opportunities stopped coming through. I went from playing 3-4 shows and gigs a week on average to no shows at all and playing at 1 church. God was starting to get my attention, naturally.

When we lack, we start facing God. I was no different. I said to God, "Alright now, I done quit my job like you asked, but you still haven't given me the big touring opportunity I wanted. I'm trying to produce more music." If I could imagine God looking back down at me, He would just be laughing at the fact that I could even fathom those words. Slowly, but SURELY, all of my bank accounts begin to dwindle. So, I decided to start working on my business to make money.

I found a get-rich-quick plan to make money. Although it didn't feel completely right, I still did it. I went through all of these trials, courses, trainings, and more to get better, but none of them worked. I was telling my family that I'm becoming a successful business owner now, but I'm just building, that's why I hadn't seen any results yet.

As I'm building the business, I lose friends, relationships, more money, enter into major debt, repossession, depression, high anxiety, and fear. How was I going to maintain how people knew me as an academically successful and musically accomplished young man to a struggling business owner with no options? I had a fear of looking like I fell off.

What hurt me the most wasn't losing resources; I knew how to survive and get by eventually. My greatest pain was losing my image. I built an idol of how I was perceived. So much so, everything I did was to satisfy and promote the image I created. I didn't want to look like I had failed. I didn't want people who loved me to question my decisions. I didn't want them to think I was irresponsible when I told them, "God said trust Him," but I couldn't yet show the results. I didn't want them to know I was in a season of drought, because I couldn't explain to them why I was there. I needed the validation of my image in order to survive.

When God calls you into a drought, He also calls you away from performing for people. I had to be freed from needing validation from the people around me.

Your spiritual, emotional, and financial wealth begins when approval is no longer your provider.

Lesson #2: When challenges arise, it is a sign that you are headed in the correct path. How you overcome the challenges determines how you move forward.

In every drought, temptation rises. When God didn't move as quickly as I wanted, I tried to justify my compromises. I went back into old parts of my life. I entertained old behaviors, relationships, and mindsets. I convinced myself that comfort was safer than obedience. I slipped into environments and habits that felt familiar, even though they were harmful to me. Because I felt God wasn't moving quickly enough, the certainty of sin felt easier than the uncertainty of Faith. Here's what I learned: every time you justify an old pattern, you delay a new season.

But, being lost, I returned to my old seasons because they felt easier. It was easier to rely on old friends for advice. It was easier to fall on old habits for comfort. Sometimes the past feels safer than the promise. I wanted to go back to what I knew because stepping into a new season with God felt like stepping into darkness without a flashlight. What I learned: Wealth, in any form, is only given to those who are willing to move forward even when it's unfamiliar.

Still lost, I wanted God to rescue me. I spent time praying, fasting, and believing for God to answer my prayer as I desired Him to answer. I wanted him to take me out of sinking water, not by boat or plane, but on a raft. I was asking for rescue when God was saying, "Trust Me."

The people around me wanted to help. Family, friends wanted to rescue me. They were available and had the resources to pull me out of drought, but God gave me a conviction about not receiving it from Him. In my journey, God ensured that he would get the full glory.

I was disobedient. I tried to take the money and support from my family and friends anyway. Literal thousands of dollars were offered to me, and God wouldn't let me take it. He wouldn't even let me receive it. Bank transfers, wiring, deposits, payments all declined. I was so frustrated to be so close to relief, but I couldn't touch it. Audibly, God told me, *"This time, it cannot come from them."* If God allowed them to carry me, I would always believe the blessing came from people, not from Him.

Lesson #3: In seasons where God is rebuilding you, support from others can interfere with what God is trying to grow in you.

Everyone reading this wants to know: When will it happen? When will my breakthrough come? When will I see results? When will I stop struggling? Jesus answers this in Matthew 25 through the parable of the ten virgins.

Five were wise, five were foolish. The difference wasn't the lamp; it was the oil. Everybody receives the same opportunity. Only prepared people receive the elevation. The foolish wanted the blessing without the preparation. The wise understood that preparation takes time, weight, patience, and discipline.

Your waiting season is not punishment; it is preparation. Preparation gives you the capacity to sustain wealth once it comes. God releases elevation only to those who can manage what He gives.

So, like the five foolish of the ten virgins, I had to learn to stop asking people to save me.

When the bridegroom came, the foolish virgins tried to borrow oil. But the wise refused. The wise did not refuse to share their oil out of selfishness, but out of stewardship.

This is where I got stuck. I was asking people to loan me what God told me to build for myself. I wanted the results, but I didn't want the preparation.

I kept blaming people for not understanding and being misunderstood. But I had built an expectation of them to pull me out. This is why when having to let go of old friends and relationships, I struggled. Because I had already outgrown them without knowing it. And if they had pulled me out of where I was, I would have ended up in drought again, because I didn't prepare for what I was being given.

Lesson #4: Your peace is part of your wealth. Protect it at all costs.

Protecting your peace is non-negotiable if you want to build spiritual, emotional, and financial wealth. Guard your mind, your heart, and your environment from unnecessary noise, toxicity, and comparison. When you maintain inner calm, you make better decisions, steward your resources wisely, and hear God's guidance clearly. True wealth begins in peace, because a turbulent mind cannot sustain blessings or multiply opportunities.

PART V - HOW GOD ACTUALLY BUILDS WEALTH

AN OVERVIEW

If you have read this far, I pray that you gained an understanding of the divine instruction of God and his will for our life to thrive and succeed.

The first six chapters of this book have dealt with the mindset of becoming. In order to turn your message into something profitable you must first be intentional about laying yourself bare before God so that he can build you up in his divine direction and order. In order to gain success in any area of your life and have that success be sustainable for you, your children, and your children's children, you must allow God to diminish you and experience necessary darkness. From the necessary darkness, God blooms you into a beautiful light where your fruit is matured and ready to be received by the community you are specifically designed to serve.

Chapter 7: The Legacy Order ™, is a deeper dive into how to be creative. As we have discussed thus far, God's will for our life is to create and innovate what he has already made good. This chapter will discuss that in the world of music creativity.

God has called me to serve musicians, artists, producers, and writers. Often, the music community is expected to pour out in excellence, but there are very few credible resources that pour into music individuals in high excellence.

This chapter of the book is specific to music. We will discuss how to be creative in music as a writer, producer, musician, or artist. In addition to how to be creative, this chapter outlines a plan for you to turn your creative gift and message into an abundance of spiritual, emotional, and financial wealth.

Many times we hear that God is one of abundance in life. However, abundance in life is more than just living to be of old age. Be very clear, yes, God desires for us to live abundantly in our spiritual wealth and emotional health; however, too often, we limit God to only be powerful enough to deliver us from crisis. We fail to consult God on how to grow the spiritual, emotional, and financial wealth he has already given us.

In the Bible, God makes no one a wealthy person. God does not bring you millions of dollars at once. God does not suddenly make you a billionaire or super wealthy person. Any entity that offers to make you a sudden or immediate millionaire, billionaire, or wealthy person in any area of your life is not of God. God operates in the process of innovation and growth. We have to trust his process first, then continue to allow Him to expand our spiritual, emotional, and financial wealth exponentially according to his plan.

In 2 Kings, Chapter 4, there is a woman who is distraught because her husband died and left their family in an extreme amount of debt. The government threatens to take the woman's two sons into slavery in exchange for the debt the family owed. All the woman owned was a little bit of oil. God did not send someone to erase her debt, give her money to survive, and thrive. Instead, God allowed her to receive prophetic instruction to take the oil, borrow jugs from neighbors, and sell it to pay off her debts and live on the remains. God allowed the process of the woman's little to make her a lot; not by giving her money or fame directly; however, he provided her with a business plan to use what she perceived as a limitation and made it her advantage.

So, should you read this chapter or not?

Yes, whether you are in the world of music or not, I would encourage you to read this chapter, because it outlines the Biblical principles God has laid out for us to succeed and thrive.

Now, I can't control whether you pick this book up or put it down. However, I can tell you that when you apply Biblical principles to your life, they will work. And fortunately, if we thought they would not work, God gives examples in the Bible on who, what, how, and why they work in any area of expertise.

So, while this chapter is going to reiterate what we have discussed thus far, we will parallel the understanding of the process specifically to the benefit of musicians. In all, any person can learn from the knowledge of this chapter, because it follows a formula for God-focused and divine success.

Chapter Seven: The Legacy Order ™

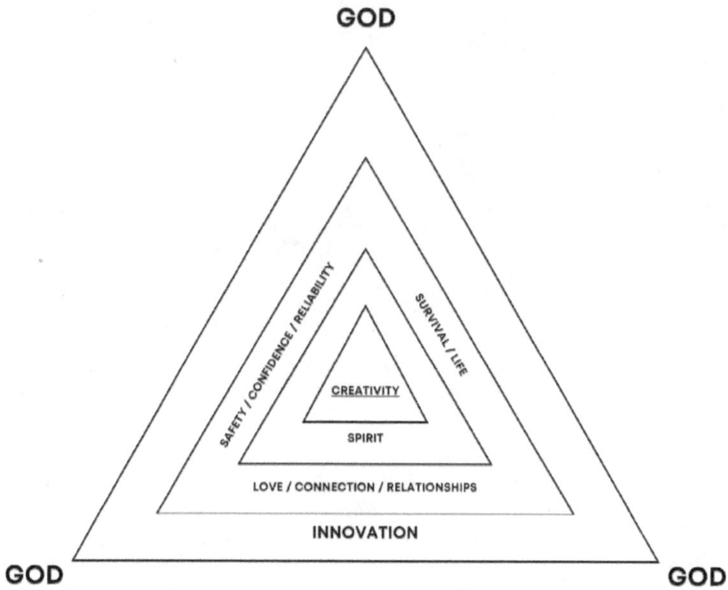

The Legacy Order ™ is a framework I developed to outline clearly how

God desires for us to use our creativity to innovate and thrive. Each side works together and cannot be separated. In so, it is our responsibility to consult with God about all things to determine where our focus should be. Now, the Legacy Order I have developed is a mirror of Genesis 1. However, I have taken the knowledge of human understanding to innovate a clear visual of how turning our creativity into a legacy is Biblically aligned. The Legacy Order ™ is a model that any person can follow to create a long lasting generational wealth rooted in spiritual, emotional, and financial gain.

Creativity

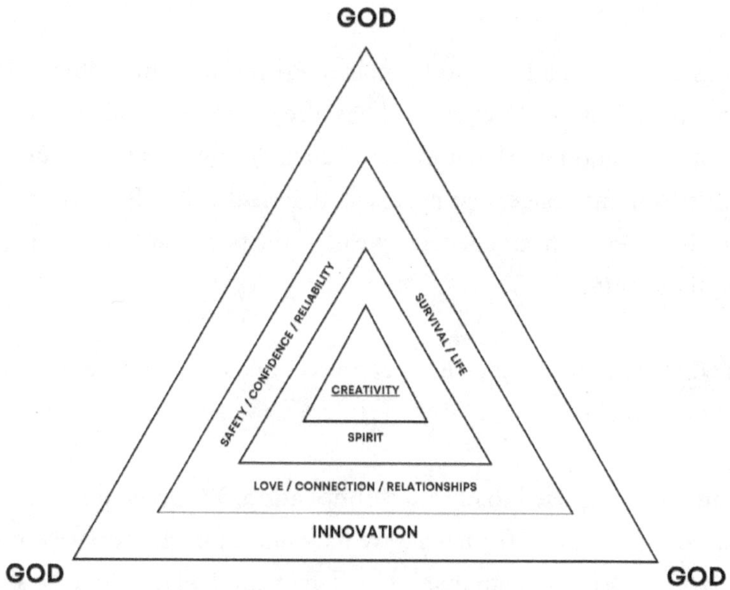

At the center of The Legacy Order ™ is creativity. Genesis 1:1 "In the beginning God created the heaven and the earth. At Genesis 1:26, "God said, Let us make man in our image, after our likeness: and let them have dominion..."

You can not understand your purpose if you do not understand the one who created you. God gives us the purpose for our lives in order of importance by introducing us to his identity first. His opening statement to us (man) is not about what he is able to do; it is about the work He has already done and intends for us to take advantage of. God creates. And after he tells us what he has made, he then makes it known that male and female are made in his image. Therefore, our purpose on Earth is defined by God in his detailing of what he is able to do.

Being that we are made in God's image, our assignment as it is in Heaven is to create and innovate what God has already made good. He desires for us to make his good work better. How do we know this to be true? If God has made us in his image, that means all that he did and declared in Genesis chapter 1, verses 1-25, and beyond, we have the power and purpose to create and do those things too.

God's will for our life is to take the resources and opportunities that he gives us and make more from it.

You and I are supposed to embrace innovation. We are supposed to grow, expand, and make more from what we have and gain. How do we know this? Genesis 9 "Whoso sheddeth man's blood, by man shall his blood be shed: for in the image of God made he man. And you, be ye fruitful, and multiply; bring forth abundantly in the earth, and multiply therein."

God's desire for our lives is not just about receiving reward in Heaven.

When people die it is insinuated that the living has gone from labor to reward or promoted to glory. While we revere a well-life lived and work completion, believing that one only receives ultimate reward in death is a poverty mindset. God CLEARLY says that we should be fruitful and multiply and bring that multiplication abundantly in the Earth, which means, we are supposed to enjoy the abundance of reward from our labor while we are still here. We are Biblically responsible to experience abundance in God's glory while on Earth. Being fruitful and multiplying is about you making what God gives you better by embracing the innovation, development, and growth of it. And when you grow it and increase, ENJOY that increase while you're still ALIVE on Earth.

What is great about the Bible is that God knows his children. And sometimes, we don't get it right away. So, he put the same message in different forms in different places from different people in order for us to gain clarity to the same thing. Genesis 1, God creates and tells us it was good. Genesis 2, God takes what He has already made good and brings to Adam an assignment to name all of the animals and creatures. God's first assignment to His image was to innovate the structure He had already provided and make it better. Adam took God's animals, which were already good, and made them better by giving each animal a name.

Creativity is at the center of The Legacy Order ™ because creativity is the center of how we should constantly live and thrive according to God's will and purpose for our life. Take what God has made good and make it better.

For any creative person, you have a gift. Whether in music, technology, mechanics, counseling, hauling, communication, or any field, you are the catalyst to making your gift make room for you in a life of wealth. The gift, talent, or skill that you have is from God. God gives you the foundation and provides you with awareness and opportunities to develop and innovate the foundation He provides you with.

If you are a natural chef; You love cooking, it makes you happy, sometimes you cook because you want to make others happy; you get lost in cutting, chopping, boiling; you can cook for hours without getting distracted; everyone says to you that you have the best dishes like none they have ever tasted. Why would you ever think that going into the culinary professional field does not suit you?

Here is our problem:

Too often, we limit what the possibilities for our creative gift can be based on what we know already exists and not the direction God desires for us to move in.

We lock ourselves into the idea that walking in our creativity is not profitable or realistic. Many times I have heard, "Don't be a musician," "You know musicians don't make a lot of money all the time," "Your day will end," "When are you going to quit and get a real job," "I don't think what you are doing is sustainable." While these statements impacted me in my early years, I chose to be obedient to the voice of God over the voice of people. In so, God revealed that many of the statements against building a career in a creative path are rooted in unawareness, fear, and simple untruths. If the first thing God does and says in the Bible is creation, why would it not make sense to focus our lives in being creative? The catalyst is understanding that your creative career has to go beyond the limited mindset of the positions you think exist for you.

In American culture, we teach our children to go to school, get good grades, and behave properly so that they can grow up and get a good job working for somebody else. From then on, they need to be obedient to the rules and expectations of that good job so that they can retire and rely on the job or a government to be their source of survival for the remainder of their life. This way of thinking is a poverty mindset. We must operate in spiritually aligned creativity to build our lives. And operating in the spirit requires that we take risks without knowing the outcome.

The reason we limit ourselves to thinking the only way to be successful in a creative career is by working for someone else or being lucky enough to get a good-paying job is because that is the amount of control we have in making ourselves successful. In the way of God, we must trust His plan before being able to see His plan completely. It is easy to work towards keeping ourselves small; however, working for someone else and having no source of income that you have built on your own puts a cap on your ability to create exponential wealth.

Now, yes, you can strategically place the money you get from a job and allow that to fund your creative career. However, you need to follow a plan so that your creative career creates an abundance of life for you. But do know this, at some point, you will have to make the big step to trust God completely and walk fully in your creative calling. God will give you the exact plan; however, it can only be revealed when you release control and move forward without knowing what is going to happen next.

God did not call His people to struggle. However, the reason we struggle is because we have to first demolish the false ideas and practices we have been taught and conditioned about God. From then, we must gain an understanding of how God truly operates and develops His children. The reason we struggle is because we want to hear the voice of God but still keep one foot in the door of control, just in case the instructions of God don't work. Doing this leads to you being in a spiritual cycle.

You're not stuck or in a cycle because you don't know better. You're stuck because you love the thing that's destroying you.

We experience pain and allow it to stop us from reaching our goals. Every decision that we make is a reflection of who we are.

You are what you do every day.

Sometimes we make decisions that are not positioned within our best interests. You have to be realistic and honest with yourself *first* about why you are where you are. You may not want to accept it but it is your decisions that have led you to where you are.

Now, if this is you that does not mean you are there forever. There are strategies to help you win the spiritual, emotional, or financial cycle you are in. If you don't know that you are in a cycle let me tell you clearly what it is.

A spiritual, emotional, or financial cycle is any hardship that you experience over and over again.

Here's how you get out it:

Let's be very clear, situations happen. We have legitimate problems, issues, and challenges. We are sick, have seemingly irreversible conditions, are powerless, broke, tired, and the list of turmoil goes on. First, you must change your mindset. How do you change your mindset? Start operating like where you are going instead of emphasizing where you are. You have to create the capacity for your new life before you actually see the results of it.

Your new life is not always a complete reset or new business and cutting people off, although it can be. Your new life can simply be living healthily. Your new life can begin with choosing to stop gossiping. Your new life can be getting a steady job that doesn't involve a world of crime or risks. It does not always have to be the most drastic thing for you to start operating in it. However, you have to intentionally decide that you are not going to go backwards.

Stop saying that you are trying. You cannot live between doing something and not doing something. You are either doing it or you're not. Living in between doing something and not doing something is a poverty mindset. Your lack of decision to do or not do keeps you in a cycle. You are limiting yourself because you will not fully commit to either side. Additionally, you allow yourself to be in unnecessary spiritual warfare because your new life rejects your old behaviors. Therefore, in order to make yourself feel more comfortable, you stay in between doing and not doing. This creates more danger because the behaviors of the old life infect the prosperity of the new life you desire. You are opening a spiritual door to hindrances that you already worked to overcome in the past. In so, living in between doing and not doing wastes financial time. You spend too much time fighting against the clock, splitting yourself between what was and what is to become, so much, that you miss the opportunity to create in the new because you have not created the capacity for abundant opportunity.

If this is unclear, let me clarify: the reason you're struggling walking into the new you is because you won't let go of **all** of the parts of the old you. In order to beat the cycle of emotional and financial lack, you need to fully let go everything of your old behavior because it does not produce wealth. And this is where some get lost or quit the process. They find comfort in between success and lack because it's gotten them to where they are. Or, many people stop here in the process because they believe what they are doing is working. What is the evidence of what you are doing being able to create an abundant life for you? I know that it is hard to release control; however, imagine how much further you could be financially if you trusted God to elevate you instead of trying to elevate yourself.

We have to break the mindset that success in a creative career is only for celebrities. We have to break the mindset that success in a creative career only happens if we get a big break or opportunity. We have to break the mindset that success in a creative career only happens if we sacrifice our well-being. That is not how God works. However, you have to break the mindset of old beliefs and allow God to build you up with an awareness of truth according to His word.

As a musician, writer, producer, or artist, you may have to let old people go that you were once comfortable with playing, producing, and working with. True relationships sustain regardless of innovating circumstances. However, if you needing to take a season away from the relationship in the capacity you once performed causes strain, that is an indication that your ability to produce for the relationship was more valuable than your well-being in the relationship.

If people you called bro, sis, friend, or family get upset because you are taking time away to grow, their reaction reveals they never valued you. Accept this truth. Understand that letting go of those people and moving forward from those relationships creates the capacity for new relationships to come and be of benefit to your creativity and growth as a musician and person overall.

People stay connected to some relationships because they fear the period of isolation. We stay under regimes and relationships we know that are not beneficial to us because we fear being alone. The reason we fear being alone is due to a need for validation of our process in becoming who we desire to be.

You have to break the mindset of requiring and desiring people to validate your process. Here is a truth:

If you are walking into a new creative life of abundant wealth, no one is going to understand what you are doing, especially the ones closest to you.

Even when growing and moving out of your old life, the people closest to you only expect the old version they once knew. If the people around you are not creating and innovating themselves, they will not understand the path you are taking to build spiritual, emotional, and financial wealth according to God's will for our life. If they are not creating or embracing innovation around them, it is more than likely they are suffering from an unawareness of truth. The truth they lack is understanding that creativity and innovation is the center of God's ordained plan for our life of abundance.

I love my parents. I know that they love me. While I do not blame my mother or father for any untruths they were conditioned to believe, I had to overcome their need for approval and understanding for what God instructed me to do for building a generational abundance in spiritual, emotional, and financial wealth. My parents did not understand me. At times, they believed I was making the wrong decisions. I was frustrated because they just didn't get it.

Many times, the approval we seek is from parents, parental figures, family, close friends, leaders, and people we trust. We week their approval because they were the ones who guided and nurtured us in our previous seasons. It is crucial to pray and practice a release from the approval of people who are not God. The only entity you need approval from is God. If you're spiritually aligned, anyone who goes against what God has written loses the privilege of the position they once held. That relationship can't benefit you anymore.

Our human side causes us to turn a blind eye on detrimental things to our process in an effort to sustain relationships that we seek approval from. We must break that mindset of allowing detrimental and damaging things to be overlooked because we feel the need to belong over becoming.

My father used to say, "A half loaf of bread is better than no bread at all…" Growing up, I believed this was true. Because I had never seen anyone around me consistently pressing for the 'whole loaf of bread.' As I gained an awareness that God wants us to do more than live, but thrive, I began to rebut my father with "While a half loaf may be better than no bread at all, I want to own the land that the bread factories sit on to make all of our bread products." And if God desires for me to own more than that, I want that too. Why have a little when God desires for me to have a lot?

We fear isolation.

God does not want us to be alone and highlights his awareness that loneliness is not good for us. Genesis 2:18 "And the LORD God said, It is not good that the man should be alone; I will make him an help meet for him."

While God recognizes that loneliness is not good for us, a period of isolation is necessary. If a period of isolation was not necessary, God would have made a helpmate at the same time he created Adam. However, before Adam received a helpmate, he was assigned work, tasks, and instructions to position himself for help to come.

A season of isolation is necessary to position yourself for help to come.

You have to position yourself *spiritually* to ensure you are aligned with God. You have to position yourself *emotionally* to make sure you are able to receive the help from people who are like-minded, without agendas that are secretly motivated to destroy. You have to position yourself *financially* to ensure the help you receive is not hindered by your lack of financial structure. This all happens in isolation.

As a musician, writer, producer, or artist, your season of isolation spiritually builds you in the divine direction God desires for you to create in. Emotionally, you have to channel the understanding of yourself to be able to develop music that reflects healthy emotional expression. Financially, your season of isolation prepares you to set your music business structure to receive things such as grants, funding, partnerships, contracts, premium value clients, and so on. Preparing yourself financially in isolation looks like registering your business as an LLC, setting up a business bank account, learning about business funding, and grant opportunities for your field.

In all, you do not suddenly become spiritually aligned, emotionally secure, and financially structured by one conversation or reading one book. However, God provides the opportunity to 1) gain an awareness of your need for change and growth 2) you accept that change and growth is necessary for where God wants you to be 3) you learn about what change is necessary 4) study the the methods to apply the change 5) plan how to implement the methods of change in your life 6) apply the methods of change to your life 7) adjust the methods to your specific life journey and learn why the specific formulas do not work for you 8) work to sustain the method that fits you. You cannot achieve this if you allow people to hinder any step of this process.

Having the wrong people around will taint your process.

The wrong people in your environment will begin to insert their beliefs that are based on their own successes and failures, and not where God is taking you. It is not that those who give you advice do not care for you or have a vindictive agenda; however, because of their care for you, it is difficult for them to see you outside their reality of what you are capable of.

Do not heed to the advice of people who have not spiritually, emotionally, and financially reached or are striving to be where you are going.

Some people say they have great Faith; however, they trust God just to the brink of them not having control. The moment anyone says they trust God but disobeys His divine instruction and order, they are moving in disobedience. There is no in-between.

People like to justify their disobedience with the action of free will. Revelation 3:20 states, "Behold, I stand at the door, and knock: if any man hear my voice, and open the door, I will come in to him, and will sup with him, and he with me." Love in any situation requires freedom. In so, God loves us unconditionally; however, He allows us to choose Him to do the divine work *on* us and *in* us. The divine work God does *on* us allows us to prepare our mind, body and spirit to receive his plan and instruction. The divine work God does *in* us allows our obedience to produce outcomes for us. Think about it like this, there is a difference between working *on* and building vs working *in* a building. Our bodies are God's building; we are his temple.

So, yes, we have the willpower to do what we want; however, our obedience to God allows us to excel, thrive, and supernaturally grow in areas we can't build ourselves. Additionally, when we take the God-direction of doing things, it ensures we are able to sustain generational outcomes guaranteed. In Revelation 3:20, God knocks on the door, but He allows us to choose if we are going to let Him in and be God in our life instead of us having control. This is another reason you must guard your confidentiality in your season of isolation.

God will instruct you to do things that do not make sense to people; however, are important to your development. Oversharing about what God intends for you to keep private (between just you and God), opens up portals for destruction that you will suffer from unnecessarily. You end suffering, because sharing details gives permission and access for people to comment and analyze.

As humans, our brains are designed to constantly make sense of our environment. That is why when we see oddly shaped fruit, a streak on a window, or look up in the sky, we make out shapes, figures, and faces from them. Our minds are constantly fighting to stay relevant with the stimuli that we receive. So, when you share instructions and actions that are specific to you and your obedience to God, you open a portal for people to make sense of your actions. In so, you are unintentionally making them your God out of a need for validation or acceptance. When you share more than you keep confidential, it is an outward display that you are searching for a need for belonging, love, and safety.

Now, we are willing to share specific details with certain people because we love them or desire love from them. However, because of their love or personal challenges, they will not understand or accept where you are going. It is essential to guard your confidentiality with Christ, because those closest to you will open wounds of your past as a means to ground you to their understanding and expectation of your behavior, mindset, and decisions. This becomes an unnecessary suffering from your oversharing as a means of acceptance.

When people are offended by your obedience to God's divine instruction, they quickly identify your lack and suffering of obedience as a defense mechanism. From those you love and honor, you may hear "Why are you doing this…just get a job"; "You have a degree and why don't you just…"; "You're a full grown…you need to just"; "Okay, you can follow your dream, but you need to do this first and your dream needs to come second…." These are all statements rooted in fear and lack of awareness. When you share about your obedience to God, they are attempting to process the reasoning behind it. If they have never seen someone truly follow obedience to God and not justify submitting to man's agenda with the free will God allows us to operate in, they will not know how to make sense of your obedience. In so, they fight against the unknown by creating familiarity. The familiarity they create is tension and destruction as a means of leveling the plot to their understanding.

Tension and opposition are more common to bring about than acknowledging the area where one lacks understanding. In other words, people would rather act a fool than acknowledge when they just don't know something. In most scenarios, people do not want to accept or acknowledge when they have been fooled. Real strength is in acknowledging the areas where you have learned and practiced untruths, because if you are aware, you can begin to grow in the correct direction.

For a musician, if you learned music by ear and used terms for years that were incorrect, it is okay to take music theory courses and learn how to read music and discuss music language appropriately amongst high-level musicians. Those around you who resist the process of innovation and growth in your musical craft will remain on a level where you surpass them simply because your mindset has changed.

Now, do not blame these people. Everyone responds to awareness differently. However, use this as a caution to understand that if you are supposed to be isolated, do just that. The only way someone will have access to defend themself against your obedience to God's will is by you allowing them to validate your process.

Once you give an individual access, it cannot be taken away.

If God has instructed you to start taking music lessons to increase your music reading ability, do so in isolation. If your actions are not impacting one's ability to function or survive, you do not need to share what you are doing with them at any rate. Guard your confidentiality.

Now, it is important to share that you are working towards something ONLY to those who are impacted by the time you spend away from their ability to function or survive. This list of people only includes your spouse, children, and anyone else you are a caretaker for. You will have to dedicate time away from them in order to grow yourself. This means that for a season, they will not receive from you in the same way they did before. Even in this, guard your confidentiality so that you may gain clarity in your own journey before revealing it incompletely. Let them know you are working on *something* and need the space to gain clarity. The process of divine isolation ensures your process and obedience to God is protected. The more you share unnecessarily as a means of acceptance, causes harm to your spiritual, emotional, and financial preparation.

Once it is time for you to be surrounded by new people with like-minded mindsets in creativity producing spiritual, emotional, and financial wealth, God will begin to surround you with people who have the knowledge and capacity to grow you. You are going to have to start interacting with people who are going where you are going and people who are where you want to be.

Gone are the days of aspiring artists, producers, writers, and musicians being able to sit in rooms or studios to gain knowledge and wisdom in music. We live in a climate where everyone wants results quickly. In so, we have minimized creative processes to produce art that is *convenient* over creating art that is *covenant.* Imagine, How would your creative process change if you consulted God before you started writing, before you opened up your computer, before you picked up your drumsticks? Sit with God first, before creating in a direction that does not serve people or push spiritual excellence forward. In so, you will have to invest into being able to sit amongst like-minded people on your path or those who have achieved what you are striving toward. This could look like traveling and paying for jam sessions outside of the state you live in; purchasing courses for instruction; joining community groups; attending business conferences; paying for 1 on 1 coaching in areas you need growth. You have to make the learning space for your field.

God will allow for you to be tested with your old life. God allows the temptation to come for you to understand that you can rely on Him and trust that He is guiding you in the right direction. You will outgrow other people's sound and behavior that refuse to innovate. Some bands, artists, and producers never grow because they find what they like to do and never go beyond their own liking and comfort to learn all of the tools and innovations that can be used to their advantage. Now, this does not mean going out and becoming a country artist to learn how to put country licks in your music; however, consult with God to explore how to learn more about the craft you are in. For those who are seasoned or believe "they've been doing this all their life," if you choose not to create or innovate, you will not reach your God intended potential. You are limiting yourself. However, if any of this has been you, do not blame yourself; simply, move forward.

Stop Blaming Yourself

You keep allowing the small slips to carry you all the way backwards. One time messing up does not justify where you are going. You have to stop blaming yourself. Don't allow one moment of weakness to mess up all of your progress. True strength and obedience to God is being able to recover from that moment of weakness. That's what the enemy hates. The enemy hates the fact that you get convicted and start doing right immediately.

As people, we are going to mess up.

In a world as corrupt as ours, temptation is guaranteed. You will always feel constant pressure to step out of God's will. Deuteronomy 14:2 "For thou art an holy people unto the LORD thy God, and the LORD hath chosen thee to be a peculiar people unto himself, above all the nations that are upon the earth." God knows that those who believe in Him are supposed to be different and unmatching of the grain of what is deemed to be normal amongst society. We are people made in God's image and descendants of His initial creation, Adam and his wife. So, God knows that if we are descendants of those who have made mistakes before us, it is of our human nature to make those same mistakes again. But don't let one mistake or a setback into your old life, old behavior, or way of thinking stop you from the entire journey of creating spiritual, emotional, and financial wealth.

If you took a road trip, a 7-8 hour drive, and 6 hours in, you make one wrong turn and say, "Well, I'm going back home, we messed up." It sounds crazy to go all the way back home because you made one wrong turn. Well, that's what you're doing in your life when you allow one mistake or setback to keep you bound. It starts with allowing yourself to be forgiven and remembering the work you have done to change your mindset and move forward.

You do not control what thoughts enter your mind.

If you think you have control, try not to think about apples.

Like I said, you do not have control over what thoughts enter your mind. However, you *do* have control over how long the thought stays there.

You have to claim your rights and control what you do, what you see, what you look at, and how you respond when the thought comes. Because ultimately, the thoughts that cause you to go backwards are just temptation.

We naturally have thoughts of failure, incompletion, anxiety, disappointment, and inadequacy. God created emotions for us to feel and understand how to navigate them. And the reason that we feel them so heavy is due to us needing to consult with God about the weight of the emotion and the responsibility we carry for us feeling it.

What we feel is a direct reflection of who we are supposed to be. Now, those feelings either are positive and build us, or those feelings are negative and we are supposed to learn why we feel the way that we do in order to help other people navigate through their emotional journeys quicker. If you always feel that there is no one around you to help you out, but you are always judged for your decision-making in trying to become better, you are more than likely destined to help people who often have no one to help them out and are judged for their decision-making in trying to become better. Your temptation is a direct reflection of your purpose.

Seems a little unfair?

Here is the good news: 1) There is no temptation that is new to Earth, and 2) there is no temptation that comes without a way of escape. How is this good news? With any challenge you are facing, there is a formula that has already proven to be successful in overcoming. Additionally, there are multiple strategies that help you get from where you are to where you want to be. So, you are asking yourself, Why do I keep messing up? Why do I keep falling for the temptations and acceptance of my old life?

Temptation is still working on you. Temptation still works on you because you haven't removed the idol in your heart. You're protecting it. Feeding it. Justifying it. And the enemy knows — you'll keep messing up, because deep down, you don't want to let it go. You find comfort in struggling with your temptive thoughts. You find relief in falling backwards. You get joy from being distracted. That's why you're in the same cycle. That is why you keep having the same desires, temptations, and compromises which ultimately lead to you being in the same cycle of shame. You go through the cycle of shame, spend some time feeling bad, get back on track temporarily, fail again, then repeat. This may be a harsh truth, but it is the reality of what is keeping you from moving forward.

Stop blaming yourself for falling into temptation, and simply, move forward.

Do something about your temptation. Be what you said you wanted to be. Do what you said you wanted to do. Some may say, well it's not that simple or easy. Well, in fact, it is. You are either doing something or not doing something. So, if you are going to succumb to your temptation, do so. However, do not waste the time of others, yourself, and God, saying that you want to change, but do not actively pursue change daily.

Ask yourself this: do you think that you need more discipline? The answer is no. You need to dethrone the thing you keep worshipping in secret. The truth is, you're not trapped; you've just built a home in the prison of your temptation. So, you feel comfortable not moving forward.

You have to be responsible for pulling yourself out of where you are. In reality, we know the one thing that is keeping us from elevating. We know the one thing that is keeping us down, yet, we allow it to keep us stuck because as long as we stay in the cycle, someone will always justify us complaining. You can always find somebody else who listens to you be weak. You're going to always have people around you when you're in one place. You have to intentionally place yourself in an environment where the people around you will tell you, "Hey, I know that hurt you. So, what are you going to do about it? What's going to change? Because if something is not going to change, then you are going to end up with the same result."

What am I saying? You do not need more discipline. You need to let the old thing go. Stop searching for people to validate your pain. Some people have told their pain story for so long that they don't even realize they forgot what they wanted in the first place. We get so used to complaining that we forget what goal we were achieving in the first place. This happens because achieving what we want is simple. Just like God's principles and instructions, getting to do what we said we wanted to do is simple. Just execute God's plan. Execute the plan, execute the vision, execute the goal. If you want more from music, you have to execute receiving more from it daily.

For the things that you want, you have to put DAILY effort into making sure that it happens. You are what you do every day. So, if you want a better relationship with God, every day you have to do what is necessary to make that happen. If you want more money, every day you need to make sure you are investing in how to make more money. If you want to learn more jazz, every day you have to invest into learning more jazz. The moment you give an excuse, the moment you give an inch of doubt, the moment you say "Well, I'mma just..." "I guess you're right..." "I hear you, but I don't know...", you have already failed at doing what you said you wanted to do.

Stop wasting time talking about the problem and how bad it hurt you. Stop wasting time writing out the vision and planning to do it, making vision boards, and having encounters on social media and chat rooms. You do not need more preparation to just start the process of building spiritual, emotional, and financial wealth. Execute the plan to become better.

Now, some of us don't execute the plan to become better because we never took the time to create the plan. If you are going to execute, you must intentionally make your goals plain. Some of us have not done what we said we wanted to do because we did not sit and write it out. We did not actually assess how we were going to get where we said we wanted to be. If you are going to execute a plan to become better, write it out.

Here is how you make a plan to become better at something:

1) Write the things you want to achieve and how you want to achieve them. 2) Execute the plan you set to become better. 3) After 1 month, before crossing into the next month, assess not for the results of your plan; however, assess your consistency of the plan within the past 30 days. 4) If you have not remained consistent, your goal is too big and unrealistic. You have to adjust your goals based on your time, ability to function, and environment.

Some musicians say, I'm going to learn 1 Charlie Parker solo every week. Or I'm going to learn ProTools this month. We get to month 2 of assessing their consistency, and they haven't begun practicing past the first 12 bars of the Charlie Parker solo. Or they haven't even purchased ProTools yet. It is not that their goals were not achievable; however, they were not realistic based on their time, ability to function, and environment. How can you learn 1 Charlie Parker solo every week if you are in school full-time for a non-music degree, involved in demanding extra-curriculars, playing at church, and gigging through the week and weekends? You cannot do that because you do not have the time. How can you learn ProTools or any DAW if you do not have a computer? You cannot do it because you have not created the ability for you to function in the DAW. So, in order to assess if a goal is realistic for you, start with assessing if you have the tools necessary to learn how to do what you want to do. If you do not have the tools to learn, start with finding every possible tool you can use to learn how to do what you are working toward. From there, create a realistic plan for you to spend time learning how to use the tools you need to learn. After that, actually use the tools, apply what you have learned by doing the thing you have worked toward. Assess your consistency at every level of learning, doing, maintaining, growing, and innovating. So, for the person trying to learn 1 Charlie Parker solo every week, it may be more realistic to set a goal to learn how to transcribe music, then practice transcribing 1 Level 1 jazz solo each month for the next 90 days. For the ProTools aspirant, it may be more realistic to first determine which computer specs meet the needs for ProTools to operate. From then, plan a financial sequence to purchase the correct computer within his budget. In the interim, study videos on the process of purchasing and familiarizing yourself with ProTools.

Do what works for you.

Do not become discouraged if what you plan to do does not work. If the execution of your plan does not work, adjust it, then execute your adjustment. Do not blame yourself for where things went wrong. Additionally, do not blame God for allowing you to make the mistake. Our frustration of not getting it right the first time allows us to never get it wrong again.

Some of us blame God for where we are. God didn't leave you stuck. He did not leave you broken. Every decision that you make is a reflection of who you are. You are what you do every day. And sometimes we make decisions that are not positioned within our best interests. The reason you keep feeling like you are messing up and don't have any strategies to get better is because you continue to choose your idol over God's way of escape. God will always provide you a way to say no to your temptation of falling backwards. We may not like what is going to help us; however, nothing you like to do is going to help you grow. A tree only grows if its roots fight their way through dirt, grime, soil, rocks, and anything that seems like a hindrance to its development.

For our lives, made in God's image, the only way we grow is by fighting our way through dirt or messy situations and problems; grime or challenges that require specific strategy to overcome; soil or unpleasant and disgusting people and things; rocks or hard things to accept that we must figure out how to pivot around in the midst of them still being present.

Temptation will not disappear. You can ask God to remove a person, thing, idol, obsession, or area of lack; however, the change needs to start with you. The change starts with you, because while God has the power to remove whatever temptation you are dealing with, you openly invite what you asked God to remove by not having nor practicing a proven strategy to keep the temptation from working on you.

God does not force us to love Him. He allows us to choose him. If you have an appetite for something that is damaging to your spiritual, emotional, and financial wealth, it is because you were never intended to touch the thing damaging you in the first place. Nevertheless, because you touched temptation in the first place, that does not make you dirty, that does not make you unclean, nor does that make you unusable. The reason you feel conviction is because you know the power that God truly holds. It is a disgrace to God for anyone to intentionally do wrong when they know how to do right. You can not blame God for where you are and the desires that you have to fail and not please him. He didn't make you love Him. He allowed you to choose Him. So, since you made the choice to love Him, you've got to love God the right way.

Spirit

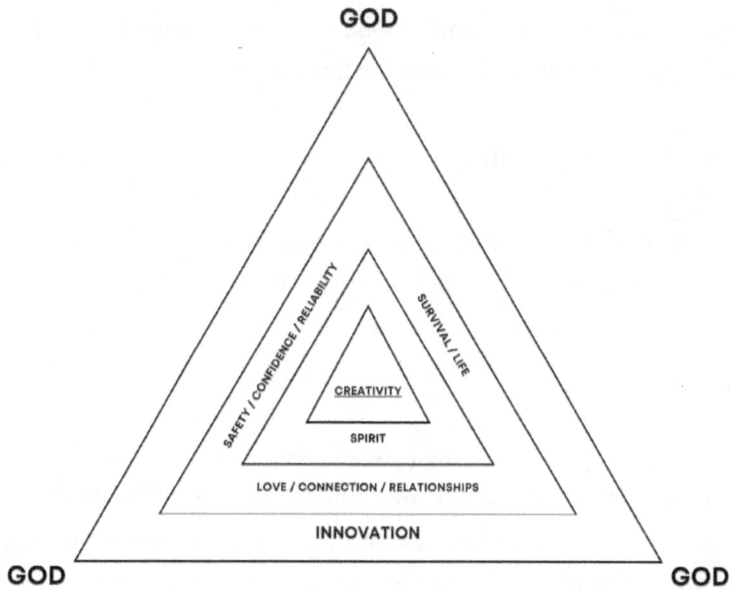

Sometimes we spend too much time trying to come up with new ideas and formulas to problems that little to few people are having. If you take problems that we already have and take a solution that already exists and make it better, with God's grace and your obedience, you are guaranteed to win.

Now, this is not to say that God only wants you to recycle ideas; however, you must know when you have been spiritually assigned to start or rebuild an industry, organization, or individuals.

Many people start organizations, businesses, and movements out of spite because they have not learned to be obedient to another person's order. God ensures that you have a formula to use before He assigns you to build or reform. However, we must stay spiritually aligned and aware in order for the formula to be revealed to us in God's timing. This is why in The Legacy Order ™, spirit is within the covering layer of creativity.

Genesis 1:1, "In the beginning God created the heaven and the Earth."

How God communicates with us is divine and in perfect order. Again, never rush through the Bible believing that there are filler words or spaces. Each text and order of translation is specifically placed for revelation in our understanding.

Just as it is written, God created the Heaven before the Earth. In so, this confirms that in our creativity and innovation, we must consult with the Heaven before we consult with the Earth. To add, the moment we enter into the Earthly realm of consultation we encounter issues. The very next verse in Genesis 1:2 says "And the earth was without form, and void; and darkness was upon the face of the deep." If we try to consult with the Earth, the natural, our individual power only, we are bound to consistently run into darkness, void, and lack of form. We have to stay spiritually aligned with God in order for Him to be our guidance through the darkness and the pathway to light.

Now, some people may try to draw parallels between The Legacy Order

™ and other self-actualization models. Here is the problem with self-actualization models and framework theories: Most suggest that a subsequent level of need must be met before one is able to achieve success and creativity. Well, this is only true if your ultimate goal is to thrive in self-esteem or self-actualization. Typically, the reason people who are not God-focused maximize at self-actualization is because there is nothing left within themselves to make better. They have no blueprint to assess their success. They are forced to make modifications of what is accepted and appropriate, because there is no perfect model to reflect if their journey is aligned and in correct order. The danger is in there being no structure or order for what is allowed to be modified in one's identity in order to be considered true innovation or fulfilling purpose. So, it ends up being multiple definitions of what progress truly looks like. Therefore, maximizing at any level of self-actualization is limited. So, those who do maximize at the peak of self-empowerment as their ultimate goal often are forced to recreate their identity as a false way to innovate self and purpose. Or, they exploit those young in the journey of truth to derail them from being able to to be creative beyond the power of self. This is why music, writing, producing and artistry about self and thriving on self does not work. You must foster a relationship with God in order to innovate beyond self and create multiplication beyond your own power. Simply put,

Your creativity must serve others.

Relationships are beneficial to our development and exponential to our power. Furthermore, being connected to one another and serving each other according to our God-fulfilled purpose is Biblical.

So, in The Legacy Order ™, why is spirit the covering layer of creativity?

Consulting with the spirit creates alignment with the direction God needs you to go in. God knows that the weight of the assignment He places upon you is great. In so, He recognizes that you get overwhelmed, because you are human. So, before revealing to us what our assignment is, God provides us with life experiences that require us to utilize strategies that help with our assignment *before* we arrive at what the true assignment is. In so, God continues to remind us that if we keep him at the center and focus of all of our behaviors and actions, He will continue to guide us.

Psalm 37 discusses what it is to be obedient to God and how the results will look from our consistent obedience in the face of enemies. Verse 1, "Fret not thyself because of evildoers, neither be thou envious against the workers of iniquity." Verse 2, "For they shall soon be cut down like the grass, and wither as the green herb."

As believers in Christ, we cannot compare our journey with those who are built on the foundation of corruption. You do not have to be a believer in Christ in order to be a millionaire, billionaire, or successful. However, believers in Christ who are obedient to God have a guaranteed formula for success and sustainability when they align their goals with the goals God wants them to have. This is why in Verse 4 of Psalm 37, the wisdom written speaks "Delight thyself also in the Lord: and he shall give thee the desires of thine heart."

When you align yourself with God and seek Him for instruction in everything that you do, not only will He give you the plan to create wealth, He will prepare you to be the proper steward and multiplier of the wealth you gain at an exponential rate due to your obedience. This happens because when you consult God in the order He desires you to consult Him with, your desires become his desire. Thus, developing a creative and spiritual alignment. In The Legacy Order ™ , consulting with the spirit of God is what covers, ordains, and provides protection and grace to our creative direction.

Furthermore, do not compare yourself to people or seemingly successful groups who God intends on destroying. Psalm 37:1-2 says, "Fret not thyself because of evildoers, neither be thou envious against the workers of iniquity.

For they shall soon be cut down like the grass, and wither as the green herb." God operates in survival, love, and safety; however, Genesis 1:28 tells us that we should not only be fruitful in life but also thrive and have dominion over every living thing that moves on the Earth.

Believers of Christ have dominion over the evil doers of the Earth. Believers of Christ have dominion over every living thing of the Earth. It is our responsibility to claim our rights as dominion over every living thing of the Earth and operate in the power God has given us to create life, innovation, and wealth. We must continually consult with God concerning His instruction, because He unveils the plan to use our creativity to claim dominion over every living thing of the Earth. This power from God includes our dominion over industries, cultures, nations, systems, governments, oppression, and any living creature.

Genesis 1:2 "And the earth was without form, and void; and darkness was upon the face of the deep. And the Spirit of God moved upon the face of the waters."

Our assignment to people comes from God. We cannot allow our assignment to people to come from people.

As a musician, writer, and producer, you must honor the craft of musicianship, writing, and producing. There are too many artists who idolize the craft and desire its benefits; however, they do not study it to honor its foundation. Being "locked in", making multiple beats in your room, or shedding with your friends is not honoring or respecting the craft. When you stay in one area too long, you create a coffin for your creativity. Yes, there are seasons where you must focus and create a system of repetition to become stronger; however, you have to study and create a system of reflection to determine why your improvement in your repetition is successful or absent. In other words, if you're always doing the same thing musically, you have to step away and study other successful musical formulas to determine why or why not your creativity is working. By doing so, this is how you respect and honor the craft. Additionally, you honor God by operating in the spirit of excellence.

Operating in the spirit of excellence will always validate you for the next level of access in your life. When you operate in excellence in all areas of your life, the effort you put in produces top-tier results. People do not care how well you played, how fancy you were, or how dope you "vibe." The way musicians are called back and requested again is in how they show up.

Along with developing your craft in music, you must show up in excellence regardless of the environment or expectation of the environment. One of the worst mindsets you can have as a musician, artist, writer or producer is believing that where you are is not defining where you are going to be. As a musician, never condition your mind to accept ideals such as "Well, I'm only getting paid..."; "It's just a local artist..."; "It's only going to be a little people here..."; "This is my crowd, I usually only play for.."; "I'm just a background..." DON'T DO IT! The way you foster relationships and create wealth from your creative talent is by showing up in the spirit of excellence in everything that you do, say, and produce, regardless of the assignment or opportunity. As a musician, you have to show up well in every part of the work: before they hear you, while they hear you, and after they hear you. How?

Before they hear you: communicate with clients and potential partners as if they are your dream client. Before the gig, performance, audition, or rehearsal, communicate with the person that is hiring you or is possibly considering working with you effectively. Respond to text messages, emails, inboxes, and calls of inquiry, even if the answer is no. As musicians, we tend to have an attitude of arrogance or pride. It is okay to be confident in your gift and position; however, it is not okay to idolize yourself beyond the point of effective communication with other people. Think about this, anyone that is reaching out to you has themself or is connected to someone who has heard what you produce. So, how you communicate before performing is an indication of how you will show up. And when you show up, overdeliver.

While they hear you:, overdelivering does not mean overplay; however, write, produce, and perform so well that your client and partners have no reason to say no to working with you ever again. Showing up in excellence as a musician, writer, producer, artist, or creative, regardless of the environment, is what opens up access for wealth to enter through your creativity. You are limiting creative wealth if you do not honor God, yourself, and the music craft by showing up in excellence. Beyond showing up in excellence, you open up the opportunity for your wealth to increase when you overdeliver on the excellence you provide. How do I overdeliver on the excellence that I provide while clients hear me? *Know the music,* study the environment of where you will be before you show up, know the artist or leaders you are under, dress appropriately for the occasion, follow the dress code and details, arrive early, know your part well, know the role you are expected to play in the environment, give the artist or leader what they ask for instead of embedding your own ideas without consent, be honest about your understanding of what is being required of you, and consistently reflect on your performance while it is happening, listen to how the artist is responding to your work, and so on. There are so many ways to overdeliver on your excellence. In your specific lane of creativity, ensure that you overdeliver on the experience you provide, so that your clients never have a reason to say no when considering working with you.

After they hear you: After you perform or work with a group, organization, or individual, you must network to create long fostering relationships that allow you to be called again. As working creatives, we all want to be called again (not by everybody though). We all desire to remain connected to growth, elevation, and prosperity. Operating in the spirit of excellence and showing up after someone has worked with you happens through networking.

When you network, focus not on the quantity of relationships; however, emphasize the quality of the relationships. This does not always mean shooting to build a relationship with the person you believe has the power to call you again. A quality relationship can be with the MD of the group, the bass player, the saxophonist. Build a strong rapport with the client or member of the group that is connected to your shared idea or vision. From then, the most important part of networking is not getting the number. After you get the number, contact information, best time to call, you need to FOLLOW UP!

Many networking relationships die because neither group nor individual follows up after connecting with each other. No, you are not required to build a friendship with everybody or suddenly start falsely categorizing members of an organization as family; however, you must overdeliver on how you connect with clients and partners after the work has been completed. How do you do this? Reach out to clients or partners of the organization a few days after the performance, between tours, a few months after the release, and so on to reflect on the project, performance, or work you both did. Use this moment to build you. Ask how well you did, reflect on what went well, ask about positive reviews. It is okay to ask about your performance with a client. As a working creative, namely one building a brand, you must be in a constant humbling mindset to discover what it is about you that allows you to be called back. You want to create the best experience possible for everyone that comes in contact with you.

Some opportunities you must decline. However, a decline now should not become a total cease in communication forever. How you show up in communication before playing affects how an organization or individual will proceed considering you again. And remember, while you may be in high demand now, seasons change every 3 months. You do not determine the market for your gift being needed. However, you do control the market for your excellence in how you produce being wanted.

No, do not idolize anyone to the point of sacrificing your integrity in order to please their narrative. Don't bow down and diminish yourself because you believe they are too big of an artist, musician, writer, producer themselves for you to approach them. However, show yourself to be the best candidate for fulfilling the client's creative need. By operating in the spirit of excellence before, during, and after a client works with you, it positions you to be the solution for the client before searching for you as the answer.

Areas of Focus

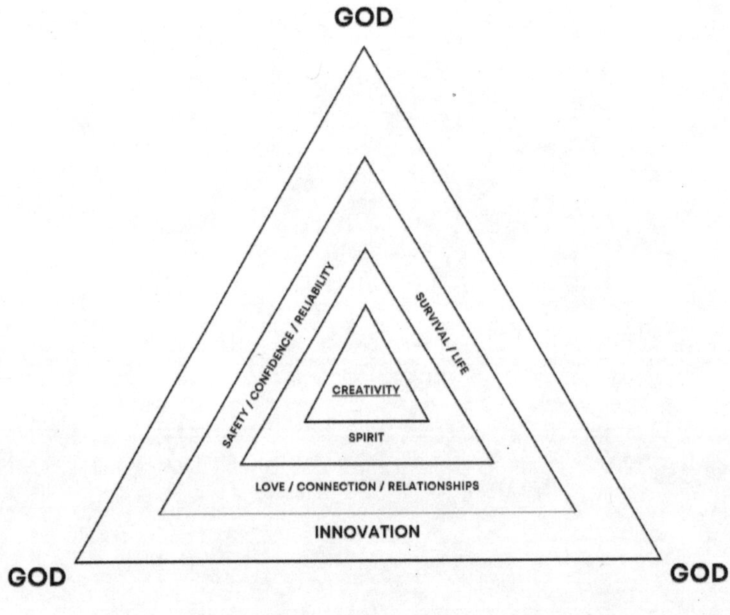

Consulting with the spirit of God aligns us with the creative direction we should move in. There are many directions that we could take in order to be famous or successful; however, there are specific principles in serving God's people that allow us to become successful and sustain in wealth.

For a creative, we must meet people at their needs and serve them there.

As a music creative, serving people at their needs looks like creating art that validates, illuminates, and creates conviction about how God desires for them to live.

In the Legacy Order ™, the outer layers of creativity and spirit are the directions we can go that are aligned with God's order and grace. We must stay aligned with God's desire for His children to live and thrive. Each area of focus is rooted in a basic human need. In so, no matter what area God gives us the grace to focus in, we are positioned to serve an unlimited amount of people. Thus, if we structure our mindset and business the correct way, we can convert the message we create based on these areas of focus into financial abundance in our own lives.

No area of focus is greater or more important than the other. What is beneficial is that each area applies to anyone. Because this framework opens endless possibilities for financial gain and creativity, we must consult with God to effectively determine the areas we must solely create or intersect.

Survival / Life

While the encouragement to live is necessary and often taught in the church, God called us to be more than living. He called us to have dominion over every living thing. So, we must determine what it is to have life and innovate within the areas God wants us to create.

Life, in its simplest form, is awareness. Everything we have, do, create, or seek is a result of life in us or around us. Life is also existence. There is nothing that has life that does not have existence. Now, this is not a philosophical discussion on the meaning of life and living. My point is, the most important characteristic of life for any living thing is survival. How do you survive?

Trees. Plants. Flowers. They must all endure environmental experiences such as wind, rain, storms, flooding, and more in order to become resilient to further life circumstances that may occur in the future. Unlike humans, plants only have two choices for survival: to live or to die. So, plants must learn how to withstand the rain so that the water from storms can reach their roots or their foundation for success. Plants must also learn how to maneuver through other weeds, insects, and more that may be systemically in place yet a barrier to the plant achieving full exposure to the sun so that it may continue to reach its fullest potential in growth and photosynthetic processing. Nevertheless, plants, trees, and flowers continue to persevere regardless of any barriers due to their being only two options for their existence: life or death.

So, a plant's identity must become resilience, empowerment, and survival to be considered functional in their environment. While some plants may seem to produce minimal success at the top of their functional existence, the roots of a plant speak for the success of its life. Plant roots are inherently a straight line. However, plants must learn how to break through different types of dirt, soil, and debris which creates the unique shape of each plant root. And even in a plant's death, their long-lasting identity must be resilience, empowerment, and survival, because the seed that it produces is a reflection of the life that the plant lived.

There are a number of theorists who believe that the human body and nature are one in their existence. Some even believe that the unique structure of the human brain is a reflection of plant roots underground. While there are many perceptions of the likeliness between plants and humans, the major difference is a human's ability to make moral, ethical, and philosophical decisions that expand their options for ways to survive. Nevertheless, the human versus nature approach continually challenges the idea that if plants can survive when specific aspects of their identity are connotatively understood as a barrier, then humans have the innate ability to find empowerment in the same manner.

Now, what does all this plant talk have to do with me as a music creative?

Create music that focuses on the innovation of life in all living things.

Just like a plant, tree, or flowers, you must validate, illuminate, and create conviction for life in people not being lived abundantly.

People wonder why music about money, riches, and surpassing is successful. The reason this music is successful in any genre is because it validates, illuminates and creates conviction of the emotions and feelings of abundance in life and survival. The songs about being able to accept that if God is able to care for plants and eagles, then we must also live abundantly are widely accepted because that is rooted in a Biblical principle. However, songs about money and riches alone being the reason one is motivated to pursue abundance is dangerous because it goes directly against God's word and principles. 1 Timothy 6:10 "For the love of money is the root of all evil: which while some coveted after, they have erred from the faith, and pierced themselves through with many sorrows."

Might I add, it is the *love* of money that is the issue, not money itself.

Creating music not rooted in the spirit of God is dangerous because it creates conviction, illuminates, and validates spiritual, emotional, and financial decision-making that is destructive to life.

We love songs about women and men engaging in violence and destruction to one's property and belongings as a means of payback for mistreatment from an individual. Songs like this validate our emotional state. It gives rise to the actions we may not commit ourselves; however, it satisfies our anger to know that destruction has been committed on our behalf. This is destructive to our spiritual, emotional, and financial wealth. Not only are we conditioning our minds to accept that destruction to one's property or belongings is the appropriate response to justify actions; however, we are also desensitizing our ability to determine what is extreme vs rational. Because it is human nature to recognize patterns and cling to familiarity for survival, when we keep consuming destructive narratives such as destroying someone's property as a reasonable response to mistreatment, we eventually start acting them out ourselves. We train our minds to believe that destruction is an appropriate answer to being hurt. If one song can have this power to reframe our mindset, consider what happens when every song we listen to shares a piece of this narrative.

So, how do we reframe this narrative and idea? In music, we must 1) validate the weight of the emotions felt; 2) create a conviction for wanting to destroy one's property and belongings for mistreatment; and 3) illuminate a strategy to heal and move forward from the weight of the emotions felt without creating further patterns of destruction.

I am not saying everyone needs to become a Gospel artist. That is untrue. In fact, I am saying the exact opposite. The genre that you write, sing, produce, or play needs to reflect the principles of God. If you write songs based on how God desires for us to live and have that life more abundantly, you will never lack in your message.

Love / Connection / Relationships

Humans naturally desire love. Love is God and God is love. It is natural to sacrifice our safety as a means of being loved. People naturally desire to belong. We are designed to thrive within communities. Having relationships is an inevitable part of high-level development. God knows and displays that there is exponential power to us being connected. However, all relationships, connections, and love begin with trust.

You can not build a relationship, connection, or fully love someone if you do not trust them. As we have discussed, trusting God is the foundation of all generationally sustained spiritual, emotional, and financial wealth. However, some of us struggle to trust God because we are suffering the wounds of trusting people.

Trust begins with vulnerability and openness. We must let something *in* to create a system of trust in a relationship or connection. Trust goes beyond believing someone will do what they say; however, in order to trust, we must believe the value in their *care* for us. It is crucial to acknowledge and communicate a lack of trust early in relationships. Most people will show how much you can trust them by how they show up for you the first time. Early cues from a potential partner, team member, or client matter. Along with consulting with the spirit of God to increase your discernment, we must improve our verbal and non-verbal communication skills to process small gestures, consistencies, and actions.

Most people will show you who they are before you trust them. We either assess our trust level too fast based on a need for change or we assess our trust level too slowly out of hope for improvement. Take what you see early and ask for clarification. From then, use the spirit of God and claim authority in your discernment to protect you from harm in engaging with a relationship, connection, or perceived love that can't be damaging to your well-being if not clarified early. If you believe that you cannot trust someone, ask them early on to clarify their gestures and actions that present to be potentially harmful.

For musicians, artists, producers, writers, and creatives, if the communication, behavior, or actions of the other music creative, partner, team member, or client you are working with do not display a spirit of excellence, 1) Ask for clarification on why they have not shown up in the spirit of excellence.

2) Assess if the small behaviors, display of mindset, and actions you see early on will be damaging to the relationship moving forward. 3) Allow them an opportunity to adjust based on what you share with them. 4) If the spirit of excellence is still not shown, make a decision to release the connection as a means of guarding yourself from spiritual, emotional, and financial harm. Never be so eager to work with someone, for someone, or around anyone that you sacrifice your spiritual stability.

So, what happens when I trusted someone, but they broke my trust?

Trust is a foundational part of our childhood development. We seek to trust and receive love from our parents first. The first successful relationship and connection we make is deemed to be one with our parental figures. In reality, this is not always the case. And sometimes, betrayal happens, and we are conditioned to accept betrayal as normalcy.

When your trust has been broken or even tampered with, do not blame yourself. You are not the reason that you cannot trust people. However, you can become the reason you won't allow yourself to trust again. You have to be honest about where your trust was broken. And openly acknowledge to God and yourself about what happened the last time you fully trusted someone and it was mishandled. From then, consult with God about the necessary strategies for you to heal from the moment your trust was mishandled. Forgive yourself for not allowing yourself to love while you were learning how to heal your trust being mishandled. Then, move forward with actionable steps and strategies to help you trust again.

What some people fail to realize is that while it can be, betrayal doesn't always look like a dramatic event. Often, betrayal happens within small breaches or repeated behaviors that lead to dramatic or key events. Witnessing these key moments of betrayal physically alters the formation of our brain. As a child, experiencing repeated betrayal creates a subconscious system for our brain to recognize betrayal as a required regularity in order to remain balanced in one's life. This ideology is built on an untruth and is out of the will of God.

Betrayal starts with behaviors like forgotten promises, lack of follow-through, or so-called mistakenly sharing confidential details of information. Once broken, trust doesn't simply return to zero. Once your trust has been broken, it often goes *negative* or into a bankrupt zone. When your trust has been broken repeatedly, you begin to expect harm rather than safety. Because our brains have been conditioned to recognize familiarity, we develop safety in a broken system of trust to a person or organization rather than addressing the root of the issue. It is easier to highlight familiarity than to do the work to become better.

To become better, you must start with yourself. Evaluate your instincts, values, and boundaries when it comes to trust. Consider these questions: When you feel that you can't trust someone, what do you do? How important is trust to you? How do you remove access to your trust?

Without self-trust, you won't know when to hold someone accountable or walk away. A lack of self-trust often leads to blind faith in others, which, unfortunately, leads to you being hurt again. In order to restore healthy trust instincts, values, and boundaries, you must understand what a healthy relationship with trust is, then work to apply the strategies of fostering healthy relationships and connections with good trust to your life.

Restoring trust is more than any individual saying "I'm sorry" or "It won't happen again." Restoring trust requires consistent, observable, and measurable behavior over time to be assessed. Sometimes people apologize *once* and expect trust to return instantly. Trust does not operate in that manner. If you decide to trust an individual or organization again, you must first assess whether the relationship is still worth investing in. Moving forward will require you to choose between rebuilding trust or releasing the connection altogether.

If your trust has been broken, your decision to build the trust relationship again or letting the relationship go is valid. However, you do have to recognize when you are the fool. Beating yourself being the fool is making the decision to recognize when repeated behaviors and a system of broken trust have caused you damage. From then, you decide to end the relationship and connection completely, because it is not beneficial to your spiritual, emotional, and financial wealth. We hold onto relationships out of hope for change or we stay in relationships to prove that our variance is successful when it truly is not.

You do not owe anyone an explanation for why you are ending a relationship or connection with them if they have broken your trust. Too often, we stay connected to family, friends, people and organizations detrimental to our spiritual, emotional, and financial wealth to satisfy our need for love. However, by holding on to anything or anyone that has broken your trust and allowing them to operate in the same capacities in which your trust was broken makes you the fool.

Relationships and connections are the foundation of exponential power in any area. The foundation of relationships and connections is trust. Trust is what creates power in relationships. Trust creates power by granting someone access to your spirit, emotions, and financial decision-making. Misusing that access of trust corrupts at a faster rate than it builds. Conversely, when you give and operate in trust wisely, you enable growth and freedom.

Now, if your trust has been breached in the past and you have not allowed yourself to move forward, here is how you begin to start the healing process: MAKE A CLEAN BREAK!

Cleanly remove every piece of the relationship in which your trust was broken as much as possible. Unless your removal impacts one's ability to function or survive, you do not owe anyone or group an explanation tp your separation for your well-being. If your separation impacts one's ability to function or survive, such as a relationship with a spouse, child, co-parent, or caretaker, then simply explain to them that you must adjust your relationship based on your need to heal in isolation. In so, you will not be able to operate in the capacity you once performed in the relationship before.

You can not properly heal from the trust of one if you simply trade the capacity of one to another. What do I mean? You can't start the process of healing from a broken relationship or connection while starting a new one first. You must heal in isolation. Let me say that again:

You must heal in isolation.

It is not that God desires for us to be alone; however, because our brain has been conditioned to seek familiarity, we will subconsciously draw parallels between actions or communication from behaviors that are unfamiliar to us. If I never do the work to heal my trust in isolation, however, I allow myself to enter a new relationship of trust, I put the new relationship at risk of failure due to an unhealed perception based on a system of thinking that trust is not true. This can look like me receiving communication as overbearing; associating care as a tactic for accumulation for revenge; or even, recognizing showing up as a threat to invade space.

If you have not done the work to heal your trust in isolation before entering a new relationship or connection within the same capacity, it is unfair to the joining end of the new relationship to bear the weight of other people's decisions that hurt you. Because of how we are designed, we will begin to unintentionally blame the person or organization for displaying signs of our perceived lack of trust without them knowing what they did to cause an emotional rift. If you do not communicate where your trust has been broken to yourself and the person you are choosing to build a relationship or connection with, you are making them responsible for knowing the rules to a game they did not even know they were playing. That is unfair to you and to them. It is unfair to you because you deserve healing.

Overall, in order to build spiritual, emotional, and financial wealth, we must take the time in isolation to learn how to communicate our expectations, then practice doing so. From then, use our strength in communication to observe what behaviors create risk for us over benefit. We must watch for one's actions and communicate our desire to strengthen or release the connection based on actions displayed rather than promises and hope for change. If our trust has been tampered with or broken, it is healthy to set boundaries that support our journey of rebuilding trust in the relationship moving forward. However, we must remain aware and consistently assess if our boundaries are set to rebuild trust or guarding our trust from being touched at all. In any light, look beyond your doubts of fostering trust and assess if you are waiting for someone to *earn* your trust, or are you expecting to be trusted by default. If you have not done the work to rebuild your trust in isolation and have not communicated your lack of confidence in the ability to trust in a relationship or connection, you then become the one who cannot be trusted. Do not blame yourself if you have suddenly become aware that your actions have played into this narrative. Nevertheless, do your work in isolation to become better. Moving forward, in new relationships and connections, monitor your response. Determine if the interactions you are having are beneficial or damaging to your ability to trust. Be honest with yourself. Do not hope or expect change, make decisions based on the actions present. If the actions in a relationship or connection do not pose additional threat to your trust, move forward. Whether small or large, if any of the actions in a relationship or connection pose damage to your trust, make a clean break to remove that connection from your life. By all means, do not ignore the little things. Communicate your emotions from the small withdrawals of trust. For the person or group you are connected to, communicate your withdrawals of trust based not on the thoughts or narratives one believes *may* take place; however, the actions that physically occur.

And to be plain, just because you were by yourself for a period of time does not mean you were actively working toward healing yourself. You have to be intentional about how you spend the time in isolation to assess your healing journey. You have to spend time by yourself, with yourself, without incorporating the validation of any other party into your process.

It is okay to receive therapy, counseling, and guidance from licensed professionals. Human behavior specialists such as social workers, Pastors, counselors, therapists, and psychologists have been trained to use scientifically proven and studied information to engage, assess, plan, intervene, evaluate, and terminate the relationship of healing. Licensed professionals have studied how to support you properly in rebuilding your trust without causing further damage. Every life coach, motivational speaker or unlicensed behavior specialist has not been trained to understand the professional psychology of human behavior and actions. Use wisdom and discernment to assess if the life coach, life builder, or unlicensed professional is rooted in studied and scientific reasoning. Be careful. Some unlicensed human behavior professionals are coaching and supporting you from a place of pain over striving toward a place of power and thriving. According to God's divine will, it is our right to do more than just create empowerment over an area of pain. It is our Biblical responsibility to go beyond self-empowerment and thrive in every area we are able to create.

In a professional relationship geared towards rebuilding trust, you will learn that it is crucial to the journey of rebuilding to identify and accept the cause of our pain. From then, we must do the work to rebuild the area that has been broken. From then, we must actively incorporate the professional skills we have learned to be resilient in our day-to-day life in order to stay in a constant awareness of the state of our ability to function and thrive. In other words, we have to get better the right way in order to stay well so that we can do more than survive, but thrive.

Thriving in life and every relationship is God's intention for our life. Now, this does not mean we are supposed to make every relationship or connection we encounter positive for our benefit. You have to decide when to cut the relationship or connection off. Doing so early, before putting anyone at spiritual, emotional, or financial risk, is what causes you to mature in building wealth. As we build spiritual, emotional, and financial wealth, longevity comes from learning how to recognize and respond to anything that harms or supports that growth. But discerning what strengthens you and what drains you begins with operating in the spirit of excellence that keeps you consistently aware of yourself and your environment.

You can only properly assess and make decisions to move forward or release relationships and connections if you are operating in the spirit of excellence *first.* Do not judge anyone who is not aware or conscious that they must improve. However, do hold a standard for what you allow to come in contact with the quality of spiritual, emotional, and financial foundation you have worked to build in isolation and beyond.

You are owed stability. You are destined to thrive. Any relationship or connection that causes you harm at any rate is a threat to your spiritual, emotional, and financial wealth. Release it. Release and make a clean, total, complete break from any relationship or connection that poses a threat to your ability to thrive. As we are covered by God, the relationships and connections that truly benefit our spiritual, emotional, and financial gain will produce exponential outcomes and align with our creative assignment.

Deuteronomy 32:30, "How should one chase a thousand, and two put ten thousand to flight, except their Rock had sold them, and the LORD had shut them up?"

There is an exponential power in our ability to make things better when we connect with others. In Genesis, God not only designs a wife for Adam based on his like-minded and shared spiritual goals; however, God also specifically ordained that his wife would be designed to help him. As Adam was completing his assignment, naming all of the animals, God caused a deep sleep to fall upon him. During his sleep, God took one of Adam's ribs and made his wife.

According to the creation of God, we are going to need help in our journey. Help will not come when we want or desire it. In fact, the help we desire may not come when we need it. However, help will be sent to you from God in His perfect timing.

According to the word of God, our help will come when we are obedient to His will and allow God the space to create help rather than us trying to make help for ourselves when we don't need it or are not ready for it. When God creates help for Adam, he is found working and operating fully in his obedience to God.

Again, with an assignment to name all of the animals, I could imagine Adam was very overwhelmed; however, he is not found complaining, yet, working in his God-ordained purpose. Your help, relationship or connection is not going to come when you most need it. Your help is not going to come when you most want it. The help for your God-ordained assignment is going to come when you are found working in it. You have to begin working and fulfilling the assignment before God creates help for you. This is an essential step in your journey of building spiritual, emotional, and financial wealth, because anyone who is worth supporting you and becoming of value to your music business needs to clearly see the foundation of your labor *first* in order to invest into a buy-in of your organization. In other words, if you want somebody to work with you or for you, there needs to be evidence that the work you are doing is worth their time to help you and be valuable to them as well.

Your business needs to clearly reflect opportunity beyond the benefits of your personal name, status, or position. You being who you are is not a selling point for someone to work with you. You claiming to be the best DJ, piano player, writer, artist, or producer with a vibe does not open the door for valuable people to want to work with you or for you. You have to ensure that you create value in working with you that people can see before you try to pitch them a job.

If you do not deliver on the value you promise to your business partners, team, and clients, you significantly decrease the financial outcome from your creativity. Additionally, not delivering on your value creates a toxic environment where partners, your team, and clients do not trust you or your words. If your words cannot be trusted, your reputation is tainted. And no one wants to work with someone with a bad reputation. Not delivering on your value creates a system of dishonesty in your environment. In so, your business partners, team, and clients will begin to engage with you in dishonor and lack. All of this is unnecessary and preventable.

You prevent dishonor and create an environment of integrity when you deliver a consistent spirit of excellence in every relationship and connection you are engaged with. Treat all people with the spirit of excellence, and you will thrive. However, consistency in the spirit of excellence does not begin with you involving other people in the learning process of how to form and run a business. In all relationships and connections, you must do the work to better yourself in isolation, then bring your better self to the relationship with skills that you have learned and are ready to apply in pushing the relationship forward. You must bring value to the connection.

If every relationship and connection you make is centered around only one receiving, the partnership becomes imbalanced. Exponential power does not happen when there is one powerful source and one empty source. Both parties must be willing to fully share and receive information to maximize the financial outcome of the relationship. As much as you are willing to receive, you must be prepared to give. Having knowledge and sharing during the process of collaboration is what creates the exponential outcome from the connection. The role you play in a relationship or connection is helping someone to fulfill their spiritual assignment. So, if you mishandle the connection by not pouring and receiving in excellence, you put yourself and that person at risk of derailment from God's divine plan. In so, you significantly decrease the financial outcome possibility.

You can not come to a relationship of any business partner or client empty-handed. Even as the client, your value must reflect in your preparation to receive. Being prepared to receive may look like you having a staff paper notebook and pencil ready when in musical environments to notate ideas, changes, or structures. In other instances, you being prepared to receive could look like carrying a hard drive for potential file sharing or chart downloading when having the opportunity to be around other producers, writers, or engineers. Displaying the spirit of excellence in receiving is also having your business organized to receive payments, payment plans, contracts, funding, potential clients, and so on. You must ensure that you fulfill your role effectively, regardless of you being the giver or the receiver. No matter what your role is in the relationship, you will not shine in every area. True strength is being able to receive in the areas you need support or a refreshed perspective. Your ability to receive regardless of you being the client, employer, or hired personnel is what creates the relationship's exponential power.

In a relationship or connection, the balance of every area is 100% and 100%. Some areas you are not good at. This is by God's design. Every encounter is designed to strengthen us. We are all good at something. However, you must be prepared to receive help in the areas where you need support. For instance, you may join a band, and the manager is struggling with branding, but is really good at organization. While you may have been hired as the keyboardist for the band, offer yourself to be a branding consultant if you understand graphics, engineering, and social media optimization. Connect with the band manager to combine their skills of organization with your understanding of media graphics to design a collaborative outcome. As creatives and more, we must use the cumulative lessons we have learned in our life to show the evidence of results that can be produced. Even if the lessons we have learned have been derived from mistakes we produced, it is all aligned with our creative purpose.

Romans 8:28 "And we know that all things work together for good to them that love God, to them who are the called according to his purpose." When you are aligned with God, nothing you have experienced or encountered has been unnecessary or unuseful. This scripture declares that while every experience may not have felt good or been good, when we are aligned with God's will and purpose, every experience works for our good. Take the lessons that you have learned, even in your mistakes, to support and serve others. Ultimately, how you serve others is what produces financial gain for you. Create a business around how you will serve others based on the creative strategies you have used to support yourself. Create a business around how you will serve others based on the creative strategies you used to pull yourself out of negative predicaments. For those who are multi-talented in areas of music, business, communication, writing, and more, create a business around you incorporating all of those skills to serve others. Take every relationship or connection to help fine-tune your skills in the areas you are talented in. From then, use your skills in every possible way to support and strengthen the connections you are a part of.

You have to go beyond just doing your job. Operating in the spirit of high excellence requires that you go beyond playing your hired role. In order to exponentially increase your financial outcome, you must display the maximum value of yourself within every opportunity that you have.

Everything you do does not have to come with money that is paid directly to you. You must be willing to offer value without seeing an immediate increase. Just like a plant, when you put a seed in the ground, you do not receive the full outcome of it the moment you place it in the soil. You receive the full outcome of the plant after you have spent time watering, nurturing, and tending to its growth. After then, you see the results of your consistent attention based on how strong the plant grows.

The process of the value you provide should be just as nurturing a plant. Although you receive the outcome later than when you put the seed in the ground, the evidence of your consistent operation in the spirit of excellence shows in the opportunities and spiritual, emotional, and financial wealth gain you receive later. So, keep operating in excellence even if the direct result you desire is not seen immediately. You limit your spiritual, emotional, and financial gain if the only way to receive your help is by paying you money directly. You must be willing to provide a service of excellence even if what you provide does not receive money via direct payment. Operating in the spirit of excellence and strengthening connections means that your business is positioned to receive an array of outcome variables. This looks like you offering a service for a client; however, accepting different types of valuable earnings outside of money.

Now, this is more than bartering. We are discussing creating strategic financial income from value in the condition of your work being provided.

You may be a violinist who plays at corporate events and charges a set rate for two 45-minute sets. Instead of simply taking your set fee and leaving, consider taking a reduced fee and requesting an extra 10 minutes to make a formal offer during the event connected to your creative business in music healing. I am not talking about throwing out a one-liner that says you do something and you hope that people are listening in the middle of them expecting you to be playing a set. This goes far beyond putting out a sign or handing out business cards. Request a space to communicate your value in a way that people cannot limit you to what they see on the stage.

By creating an array of outcomes for financial gain in your business, you are establishing a connection that is spread over time. Be willing to accept variable financial increase, the connection you establish and operate in increases your accessibility, expands your community reach, and multiplies your financial gain.

Your partnership as the client, producer, employer, or hired personnel allows your work to remain relevant to every other encounter your partner is connected to. When people are working with you, they are consciously aware and focused on your relationship. So, by nature, when the people we are connected to go to work with others within and close to the time of working with you, your work will seemingly be the most relevant to either consider or bypass.

Let's say I recently worked with an incredible singer who consistently delivers well and shows up professionally. If someone asks me for a recommendation for a singer—and what they're looking for matches her profile—I'm naturally more likely to recommend the recent singer over someone I haven't experienced in a while. Why? Because like all people, we don't just remember what you do; we remember how you make us feel.

Working with the incredible singer who showed up in the spirit of excellence makes me choose them because I can attest to their work, their character, and their consistency *right now*. Meanwhile, I can't confidently speak on someone I haven't worked with in a long time, simply because their current level of excellence, professionalism, or growth is unknown to me.

That is the importance of social media. You have to create accessibility to your value in its most current state. Showing up consistently online keeps you on people's minds, reaffirms your professionalism, and reminds others why you're worth recommending. So, by posting how you operate in excellence, when the opportunities for potential growth arise, you have created an accessible library of demonstration to confirm your skill, ability, and talent. Additionally, displaying your work in the media ensures you are not forgotten in the field.

In today's climate of media, there are countless musicians, artists, producers, writers, and so forth who share their highlights. While it is exciting to share highlights and moments of high energy in media, it is rare to see creatives emphasizing professionalism and consistency. Your content gains attention when it serves people's pain or desires. Your content is more likely to receive likes and views if people are able to make an immediate connection to the pain you are releasing them from. Videos and media that have the most engagement are popular because there is a community that is able to share a common interest with the narrative of the content. The most successful content is highly engaged because people are able to connect a part of their life with the content they are watching.

Content with pets, cats, and dogs doing funny things are popular, because a large community of people are able to draw a real-life connection to a pet, cat, or dog that displays the same or similar behavior in their own life. Content with pets is relatable and highly engaged, because pets are often forgiven for their actions and irresponsibility. Because we desire acceptance and love, our brain associates the acceptance of a pet with the need for love within ourselves. Because a need for love is a basic necessity for life, we draw these similarities unconsciously. With the excessive amount of stimuli our brain receives from media, we have built an unconscious survival system around identifying what is beneficial to our existence and further development. Within seconds of a video or any content we consume, our brain determines if we must continue to listen and engage to support our survival.

If we have been struggling to cook or been unsuccessful in the kitchen in the recent past, hearing a video hook or seeing a thumbnail that outlines '30 Easy Recipes, 30 Days, Under $30' becomes attractive to us, and we almost instantly engage because our brain is seeking to find solutions that release us from the pain we experience in order to survive. So, music creatives must develop content that serves the pain and needs that people and communities must be delivered from.

Videos with musicians who are chopping, playing funky grooves, and layering are not only popular because the music and emotional energy are high; however, those videos release a specific community from pain by creating a reality that a high level of success on that instrument is tangible. We make an association that if what we are watching is real, then it is likely to be transferable to our own reality. This is where opportunities meet advantages when it comes to artificial intelligence in music.

If our brains create a reality that we are able to produce and create at the same rate as an AI artist, producer, or writer, then we are pushing our mental capacity to a higher potential as a means of survival in our community. So, it is key to embrace the innovation of artificial intelligence or any other tool that is developed, because it creates a benchmark for our creativity to flourish. Additionally, having an AI music companion is no different than the days of being in a studio, room, or environment with other musicians, writers, and producers during the creative process. In those times, each music creative contributed to the ideas, development, and community of the project being worked on. While AI companions and any other tool that is developed for our innovation does not fully connect our human emotions accurately, it is our responsibility to provide as much information as possible to the AI or tool source for it to produce the best outcome. The way we promote the best outcome for AI music production is by inputting as much information as possible about the emotions, feelings, needs, and desires of humans into our prompt. Even if the results generated are not what we desire or feel connected to, we can use those results to help us recognize what elements of music do not work to portray the emotion, feeling, and need we are trying to convey. In the media and content we present, AI allows us to properly gauge and assess authenticity. Our attention is our greatest currency. So, to make a connection for survival, we consume content that is geared toward promoting us from staying marginalized.

To promote further identity, the reason we share content with our friends, family, and followers is to promote our image in cohesion with the message associated with the content being displayed. In other words, we share content that makes us look good and aware. This may look like us sharing content with information about resources that support underfunded, marginalized communities. Sharing information or content in this category allows people to feel connected and elevated by allowing themselves to be a liaison to a community and shared experience. Additionally, content that supports marginalized communities validates the emotions and feelings of the people watching to help them feel seen or confirm uncertainty they have had in their own life. People consume content that helps them realize their assumptions in their reality are not false. In so, sharing the content that supports marginalized communities allows us to be the representation of alignment with releasing people from the pain of uncertainty.

So, as it applies to love, connection, and relationships, through the content we share, how we show up, and communicate, we must do all in excellence. Operating in excellence promotes a foundation for success in spiritual, emotional, and financial wealth. When we can clearly be seen as an individual, business, or community representative that is aligned with helping a community survive and thrive, we become the connection to a solution for any problem people are having. When we do the work in isolation to position ourselves for an effective collaboration we create a solution to exponentially increase the financial outcome from the relationships that we engage.

Safety / Confidence / Reliability

Deuteronomy 32:30, "How should one chase a thousand, and two put ten thousand to flight, except their Rock had sold them, and the LORD had shut them up? "

As discussed, fostering relationships exponentially increases our financial outcome. In addition, our financial reach is broader when we aim to serve communities at large rather than individuals. Serving communities is not greater or less than serving individuals. No matter who you serve in excellence, it requires the same amount of focus. However, the human need for acceptance in community coincides with our need for protection.

We find safety, confidence, and reliability in the communities we choose to identify with. Safety is a basic need for human survival. Security allows us to thrive in spiritual, emotional, and financial wealth.

Building security, safety, confidence, and reliability is most sustainable when you first align your needs and desires with God. Consulting with God about the direction of your journey allows you to be confident in your decision-making. When you are aligned with God, you will make decisions that do not make sense in the moment, yet they make perfect sense in His plan. Consistently asking God for direction builds our confidence, whether we can see the results or not. Just like Faith, our life and consistency must become the evidence of God's power and strength. Our life is the evidence of things unseen. In so, we must be delivered from the approval of acceptance in communities to build safety in our journey with God.

The reason we compromise our journey and fall short to the obedience of God is because we find safety and comfort outside of divine instruction. How does this look? We may submit to the desires our family has for us to work in the family business, stay connected to a specific resource, or heed to the pattern of family decision-making in order to stay in alignment with our family's goals and vision. We must be freed from the acceptance of this narrative. While we find safety and confidence in the familiarity of family wisdom and instruction, it is not aligned with the will of God to its fullest potential for us to thrive spiritually, emotionally, and financially, if the instructions have not and do not align with creativity and embracing innovation. This is a hard pill to swallow at times because the only success we may have seen close to us has been associated with limited beliefs. While many of us have had some success, the reason God has to strip us bare before building us up is, because we have been raised and taught a system of survival based on the abilities we have within our own control. This is dangerous. Limited belief over time becomes untruth. And if we are not delivered from the untruths that we are raised in and conditioned to believe, we will suffer.

So, why do people stay? Why do we stay in systems that have proven they do not benefit us? People stay inside of systems and untruths, because they find safety, confidence, and reliability in hope for the systems rather than evidence and results of the system.

You cannot stay stuck where you are based on hoping that the system will change in work for your benefit.

If you do not actively work to change what is happening as a result of the system, while you may complain, fuss, or fight, it is a waste of time if you are not making changes to find confidence in the system being designed not to work for you.

If everyone in your family has pursued a career in business, consider what element have they not incorporated or emphasized that has caused a lack of success. Vice versa, for the businesses that have been successful around you, consider the element they have incorporated or emphasized that has caused them to thrive. Every business, idea, and belief that works has fruit of evidence that it is beneficial. However, if the system continually proves that it does not work in the benefit of a community, then the fruit it produces is not good.

It is insane to expect something different from anything if the inputs are the same. Beyond corruption in government, political opinions, systemic racism, marginalized communities, underserved groups, and more, we keep ourselves stuck when we rely on the hope that our old mindset will still work, even though we have refused to change it.

This is a difficult reality to accept. If you are stuck in financial lack and not operating in the abundance God specifically instructed us to live in, you share a poverty mindset with people who are poor and have less.

There is no specific dollar amount that equates to wealth. Wealth is not associated with six-figures, millions, or billions. There are still people who make millions of dollars living from check to check because they have not aligned themselves with the spiritual, emotional, and financial wealth principles of God. However, when people find confidence and rely on the wealth principles of God, their abundance is able to be sustained. The wealth principles of God are more than just building a specific dollar amount in a bank account or business. The wealth principles of God show us how to build wealth, sustain it, and multiply it. However, the most important structure we have when our mindset, vision, and practice are aligned with God is that we are able to create wealth without diminishing others for our personal benefit.

There are many systems, businesses, and organizations that have created high amounts of dollars; however, they are unreliable and in the face of corruption because their increase is based on the downfall of others.

Any entity that has to diminish another in order to promote itself is not of God.

We were designed to have dominion over every living thing. Dominion is control over the environment. We are not superior to every living thing. Superiority implies that one's purpose is more important than a lower ranking, non-equal. We have dominion over superiority, because every living thing serves a purpose that is necessary for other living things to thrive. As believers, we have safety in being able to create without diminishing others, but building communities. Deuteronomy 32:30 emphasizes the power of connecting being able to create exponential wealth increase. In the latter, the scripture states, "...except their Rock had sold them, and the LORD had shut them up?"

The only way we will lose the wealth we have is if some component of our wealth has not been built on the principles of God and His timing. God desires us to be obedient right at the moment He gives us instruction, because His timing produces other opportunities to open. When building a business, creating, or innovating, we must live in the confidence of God's word. The primary question or concern we have when building spiritual, emotional, and financial wealth based on creativity is 'Will this work?'

Even as strong believers, we enter into moments of doubt because we have not seen the results of the full promise yet. And, you will be tried by the people around you. Those around you will ask "Why do you continue to do something if you are not able to see the results?" "Why are you so adamant about a vision and obedience to God and it hasn't worked yet?" They will ask, "You've been doing this for some time, why don't you just do something else as the main thing and put your creative work secondary?"

If God has not specifically instructed you to do it, don't do it. If you are not sure if you are hearing from God clearly you must remove something in order to create capacity for his answer to be revealed. You must fast from anything that takes your attention away from being able to hear God clearly at any moment of the day or night. So, while things we may be distracted by include sexual activity outside of marriage, overeating, and excessive social media, these are not the only actions and mindsets that prevent us from being able to hear God clearly. In certain communities, we choose to demonize specific categories of sin as a means of judgment; however, we all fall short of the Glory of God. Therefore, we must repent daily for sins known and unknown. Additionally, James 2:10 states, "For whoever keeps the whole law and yet stumbles at just one point is guilty of breaking all of it". This verse emphasizes that any single sin can be enough to make a person guilty of breaking God's law. So, a white lie is just as bad as murder in the eyes of God. As humans, we hate to accept this truth, but all sin is detrimental to our well-being and ability to thrive in spiritual, emotional, and financial wealth. In so doing, we must also fast from things like sports, gossip, cursing, overspending, mismanaging funds, spreading false truth, emphasizing lack, and more. Removing these things from our life allows us to hear God more clearly and receive the clarity for instructions in our living.

Furthermore, when we are building a life in spiritual, emotional, and financial wealth according to God's principles, we must become a reflection of the word of God over being a reflection of 'the word of God+limitations based on conditioned belief.'

You will be called arrogant. You will be called different. You will be judged by those who are unaware and lack a confidence in God's authority bestowed within us.

In so, we must become free from the behaviors and actions of groups of people that are not where we want to be. In other words, when you are building wealth, take the actions and behaviors poor people do and do the exact opposite. When you are building wealth, take what poor people believe and think the exact opposite. When you are building wealth, take what the wealthy do and believe, and engage in those things. It is that simple. So, if you know musicians who are wealthy in spirit and finances, pray every day before they play, do that. If you know local artists who talk about 'getting money' and negative behaviors in street culture that are not spiritually, emotionally, and financially successful, do the opposite. We have to build confidence and safety in our obedience to God. And at all times, what we must do is simple. While it may be difficult, anything that God asks us to do will be simple. If we find it complicated, it is because we are inserting too many of our human emotions and doubts into His divine instruction. When we thrive in the safety of God's word, it does not matter what we look like. There is nothing additional you have to explain or do to satisfy God and receive abundance on Earth outside of being obedient to Him.

The reason Eve was deceived by the serpent was that she began to believe a narrative that there was something additional she had to do in order to be closer to God and fulfill His will for her life. God had already instructed Adam and Eve to be fruitful and multiply, and there is only one place they should not go.

We can be deceived by one thing that ultimately keeps us from fulfilling God's instruction in His timing. Depending on who we are and our life experiences, the one thing holding us back is different; it could be doubt, anxiety, carelessness, lack of attention, or even uncertainty. Understand, there is nothing additional we must do to please God or be more like him outside of being obedient to His will and instruction. Anything that goes outside of us being obedient to God and His instruction must be completely removed from our life. It is a hindrance to spiritual, emotional, and financial wealth. Our safety and confidence must rely on God's protection.

When we are creating music based on the safety, confidence, and reliability we need to survive and thrive, we must validate, illuminate, and create conviction. Validation, illumination, and conviction in safety, confidence, and reliability are songs that discuss the protection and confidence we must have in our success, beliefs, and journey, regardless of any outside opposing nature. Once again, I am not saying that everyone should become a Gospel artist or producer. In fact, I am saying the exact opposite.

Regardless of your genre, creating music that validates, illuminates, and convicts our need for safety includes songs about claiming our right to an awareness of spiritual, emotional, and financial wealth. We must take areas where people have lacked and develop music around strategies for them to heal. Write and produce music that validates people's emotions for the pain they have experienced, create a conviction for not claiming the rights we are owed in spiritual, emotional, and financial wealth according to God, then, in the same song, provide a strategy for healing from the pain.

What Happens If You Stay In Any Area Of Focus Too Long

It is questioned why CCM, rap, and other rapidly grasped genres are gravitational. There is only one reason why music is grasped quickly. Here it is: The message is clear.

The reason people gravitate to music of any kind is due to the spiritual, emotional, or financial message being clear to understand. In so, people are more likely to consume other pieces of creativity from an artist, writer, or producer if the narrative they continually speak on is relatable to one's life. The reason CCM became highly successful is due to most of its songs' messages based on the narrative of thriving. While songs of overcoming and survival are necessary, life is broader than the ability to survive. God has ordained that we thrive in abundance and we are to enjoy the abundance we create here on Earth.

Much of the music industry is oversaturated with material about negative feelings and emotions. Many songs in Gospel, R&B, Pop, Hip-Hop, Rock, Jazz, and so on are about overcoming struggle, maintaining power, restoration, cheating, anger, anxiety, and irrational behavior.

The reason we sing and enjoy these songs is due to the emotional connection they make us feel. We feel validated and understood by the lyrics and musical production intent. Now, how we consume music is neither about white art vs Black art. Nor is music consumption about new school vs old school; however, music that is highly consumable is music that discusses life in abundance on Earth. The most successful songs discuss thriving in an area of focus related to human need. For example, as it concerns *survival/life*, songs about preparation for a season of betterment are highly successful because people are able to make a connection to their journey of preparation. As it concerns *love/relationships/connection*, songs about experiencing high levels of awareness in love and feeling connected are successful because people are able to draw a parallel to the need for belonging and romantic, platonic, or family relationships in their own life. As it concerns *safety/confi dence/reliability*, songs about assurance in things that are designed for us to live abundantly are successful because people and communities are able to connect with the same source of reliability discussed in the music. This is not a theory, it is a proven fact. The Bible clearly outlines in Proverbs, "For as he thinketh in his heart, so is he..." People consume what aligns with their thoughts and beliefs.

In writing and production, the intent of the song starts with the writer's and producer's motives to create. If any music creative is not positioned in spiritual, emotional, and financial alignment, their disconfiguration reflects in the work they produce. Now, because we are made in God's image, this means that the range of emotions we display are going to reflect some part of us. In so, we reflect pain, hurt, disgust, anger, and more. While these are necessary emotions to produce powerful pieces, if we do not offer a strategy out of it, we are damaging our listeners by reinforcing that pain, hurt, disgust, anger, and more are the only ways to be successfully creative. Additionally, we are conditioning ourselves that we can only create from a place of darkness. As an artist, writer, producer, or musician, this limits you to one space of relevance to human existence. You must expand your creative reach by writing, producing, singing, playing, and performing music that is relevant to every part of the human life.

Energy can neither be created nor destroyed. Energy is only transferred from one source to another. So, when artists, producers, and writers sing, perform, play, write, and produce, their emotional, financial, and spiritual energy is transferred into their work.

Our ear canal is only 1mm from the brain. 1mm is less than the thickness of the tip of a pen. As consumers, we often place sounds or music close to our eardrums by way of earbuds, headphones, monitors, in-ears, or loudspeakers. I am not saying take the music away from our ears; however, be aware of the energy that is produced and reiterated into your brain. The brain controls every function of your body. If a song or music being played goes into our ears, the first place the energy, message, and authority of the song hits next is our brain. Our brain makes a connection with the song and seeks to settle into the familiarity we are able to associate with it. So, whether it be the first time we heard the song, how the song makes us feel, where we often perform or rehearse the song, our brain associates songs with our experience.

Some people are extremely talented and are available; however, they often do not play or have the opportunity to play and perform because the energy they produce is not attractive. They can hit every note, play any lick, vocally run from New York to California with ease, but their energy does not translate to a positive experience. Many times, it's because they are not emotionally, financially, or spiritually positioned in wealth.

I often joke to my friends about choir virtual instruments and plugins sounding bad. Now, do not get me wrong, there are some excellent and unimaginable products that reproduce human sound. However, it is undeniable that while you can capture excellent samples and recordings, there is nothing that accurately recreates being in the room of live human production. Even as a performer, while practice, rehearsal, and professionalism ensure a consistent show, every production is different. The reason is due to human energy. Humans feed from energy and it impacts how we consult with the spirit world.

Seeing someone crying can change how a drummer is hitting a snare. A 7-year-old being at his first concert, looking up at the stage, can impact the intensity a bass player slaps. A pianist having a baby in the audience tries to play his soft volumes more like a lullaby. A drummer hits the snare a little harder to make sure he's not too soft because he went hard in the gym earlier in the day and can't really feel his arms. These all seem like subtleties; however, combined with the individual impact from each performer or player, the dynamic architecture changes the overall outcome of the performance.

Music and creativity are a reflection of human life. Because we are multifaceted people, our seasons of focus cause us to perform in one light over others at times. While this may seem like an imbalance, there is a beauty in being imperfect. In so, music, creativity, and art are imperfect.

Once again, it is important to embrace tools such as AI that promote structure and continuity. However, where AI and other specific tools are designed to solve problems, they present a limitation. Because tools are designed to help us in a designated area, they create an additional problem elsewhere. AI promotes structure and continuity, but it does not always account for imperfections. As humans, we can not explain why, in certain pieces, the drummer playing in a different time signature than the rest of the band feels good, but it does. We cannot explain why an 808 being almost a half step up from the key of a song while the vocals are flat, but everything else is in tune works, but it does.

The list of isolated components that we could label as imperfections goes on and on; however, as humans, we develop a subconscious awareness of these imperfections and use our creative talent to bring balance to the energy being produced. Here, it is important to recognize that in order for us to bring a balance to our creative art, we must have a vocabulary that allows us to make decisions that promote balance in our production. For musicians, artists, writers, performers, and producers, we must have the musical vocabulary that allows us to make better musical decisions.

When performing live or in-studio, we can feel when the energy is off. Here, we fall into a fight or flight stage. In a fight response, we address it openly to come to a compromise, OR play more licks, do more runs, sing louder to achieve some sort of balance to the energy not being where it needs to be. In a flight response, a musician may retreat from correcting the energy disposition as a means of protecting their own space, OR they make no adjustments to their musical part in an effort to claim no accountability for the unsuccess in the performance. Any one of these responses can be dangerous and potentially more damaging to the performance. Responding in a fight reaction in this manner can result in misunderstanding if not handled appropriately based on the environment you are in. Simply playing louder or doing more when the music requires less can become a distraction. In a flight response, this becomes problematic because retreating or failing to openly contribute to the disposition of musical energy allows the musician's character to be perceived as unaware, unattentive, and uncaring. How do we fix this? The solution is what separates the big boys from the little boys, the women from the little girls.

Consult with God first about the situation. Ask God for clarity on what is happening, why things do not sound or feel right, and how do I properly address the energy disposition in this moment. Now, you won't always have 40 days and 40 nights to consult with God about a problem. This is why you should continually seek God's face daily and keep your emotional, financial, and spiritual space clear to receive from God at all times. Why? Sometimes we need an answer from God before we figure what to ask him. If we are continually positioned to receive from God and hear his voice, he will give us the answer before we even finish asking the question.

Second, a musician must have the effective musical language and skills to add tastefully without creating further interruption. Every lick does not fit every environment. Many times the musicians who perform globally are chosen because they have positive energy and they know how to play licks, runs, and chops; however, they thrive in doing their part. The most popular songs performed require each member of the band to simply play the part exactly how it is. When the energy builds, the time presents itself, and it is required or expected of you to do so, *then* you add chops, licks, and runs tastefully without losing the integrity of the piece you are performing. If it is not required or expected of you to add based on the environment you are in, you should refrain from doing so. Let me be more specific. The chord change, transition, run, or chop you practiced all week and sounded good to you and may have even sounded good in rehearsal, is not needed if it will cause damage to the musical experience of the environment you are in. Let me be more specific. Because you spent all week playing a shout bump and it killed in your bedroom or another church the week before, does not mean play it at your church for the 8 am service. If the energy is not within the room for that to happen, you forcing it there will be more of a distraction than an embraced sound. As for other genres outside of Gospel and church, saying, "They're drunk, they won't remember, we can play what we want…" is not an excuse to compromise musical integrity. Yes, have fun while you play and perform; however, you must always be attentive to the leader, whether it's your choice for them to be in charge or not. Additionally, be attentive to the audience to determine if what you decide to add is truly elevating the energy of the band, group, and circle, OR are you attempting to create a moment that solely elevates yourself as the individual saviour for the energy loss. This includes your choices as a singer as well. Sometimes we go on autopilot with our chords and runs, instead of developing our craft to increase our musical vocabulary for determining what can be tastefully added.

In the age of social media content, some of us musicians keep the cameras up and sacrifice the energy of the room in order to create a moment for video. While your 60-second clip may gain a good number of likes or views, consider what your changing of energy to the room truly did for the entire experience of the environment you were in. Now, this is not always spiritual;

however, God, in his infinite power and wisdom, can use any moment to help anyone grasp the message he wants them to receive. Consult with God about everything that you play and perform. Yes, even consult with God about the R&B, Pop, Rock, Jazz, and other genres you play. God knows everything that is in the world and of the world. God created man in His image. So, why do we receive convictions from playing genres outside of Gospel? Ask God, then self-assess if you are operating in a learned conviction. Additionally, ask God, then assess if you have the grace to play the genre you are playing. Lastly, ask God, then assess why you are playing the genre and using your creative talent the way that you are and the spaces that you are in. If you do not consult with God *first* about all of these things, you run the risk of wasting time and resources in the wrong area that is not building your development. And do know, just because you are making money or receiving some level of success does not mean you are operating in your God-intended purpose. Remember, hot sugar looks like warm oil until you touch it.

Nevertheless, think to yourself, "Would I play this or take it there if the camera were not up?" "Would I try to create this moment if my family member were not in the audience?" "Would I shift the energy of this environment if I were not performing with someone I am close to?" You have to remain conscious and aware because God can use any environment, person, place, or thing to send a message. You do not want to be the reason a message is missed because you did not creatively contribute to the energy of the music performance being elevated. And elevation is not always congruent with playing louder, being louder, or doing more. Many times, musical elevation is rooted in each specific part playing its role effectively. For a band, this may mean playing a more simple kick pattern in the drums, no runs in the vocals, darkening your sound as a horn player, pulling layers of patches back on keyboards, or moving to a lighter skin on percussion. In the studio, this may look like going outside of your normal vocal chain and simply adding just basic EQ and compression, singing in your head voice a few inches away from the mic to keep a consistent input into the microphone, or using a different snare that sits in the mix better based on the song. However, you can only make these changes and have them be effective if you have done the work to study your craft in preparing a musical vocabulary of decisions you can make to elevate energy. In all, you have to be aware of the energy you produce in performing and creating and consider if the choices that you make are elevating the specific environment you are producing for.

As a musician, writer, or producer, after consulting with God, the way you make good choices to elevate the energy of the environment you are producing for is through communication. Improving your communication skills will increase your wealth in every area. In order to contribute to energy elevation while writing, producing, and performing, you must have the musical language in music theory to effectively understand what is needed for the moment and how to communicate with others the necessary path for elevating a cohesive energy in the music.

Let me say that again, because I know that I might have just lost a few readers. *You have to learn music theory.* There are many free, unpaid courses on YouTube and different site platforms. Additionally, there are many local universities that offer music theory education courses online and in person. Last, there are private lesson instructors who teach just theory lessons. Music theory is important to learn because it is a unified language that translates musical understanding across all human speaking languages. Music theory allows an English-speaking musician to understand French, Western, African, or regional-based music without having to speak the composer's language. Beyond this, music theory allows musicians to communicate an effective, unified language across genres regardless of the musician's specific background.

Now, beyond theory, you have to understand who you are communicating with. A musician, writer, artist, or producer may not have the level of music theory knowledge to explain what they desire. In any situation, ask how the artist, leader, bandmate, or partner receives communication best. For those who may not understand music theory or are not advanced, be honest. If someone is communicating with you musically in a way that does not make sense to you, be honest about your understanding of what is being requested of you. And as the lead in a musical group, partnership, or organization, you have a responsibility to first recognize if it is your assignment to lead. Just because it is assumed that you know the most does not mean it is your grace to be the leader. Nevertheless, as the lead, you have to be able to communicate with other creatives and artists about what you need or desire beyond just a "whoom" or "dash" or "and then hit at the end." You have to do your diligence as musicians, performers, and creatives to study the craft of your instrument and environment to understand what is required to elevate harmony.

Now, some things you will not know or be aware of how to explain due to the nature of the instrument or art not being within your expertise. For example, in-studio, you would not know how to explain placing a parallel compression on a drum bus, then sending that mix to a plate verb. However, you must work to develop your explanation beyond a statement such as "I need the drums to sound like a boom, boom, clack..." While seasoned professional mix engineers have the knowledge to translate your 'boom, boom, clack,' working to increase your knowledge of the music craft allows you to communicate with other musicians, artists, producers, and writers about what is musically needed or desired. While you may not be deep into the field of mix engineering, it is more understood and accepted if you are able to make statements such as "It feels like the drums are getting lost in the mix, can we make the entire drum kit sound bigger overall and add space for them to ring." All three statements are conveying the same message; however, they are better understood if you are using the language that is spoken within the craft. For every component of music and the environment you are spiritually assigned to work in, increase your knowledge so that you are able to communicate the language of the craft effectively.

Music theory is the avenue through which musicians are able to understand the details and rationale of what they hear or play. And once again, learning, studying, and knowing music theory is necessary in the development of improving your music creative craft.

There are many musicians who watch and listen to other musicians on social media, long-form video platforms, and more, to wonder how or what is being played or performed. Here's the secret you may not know, I'm going to tell you.

Great musicians study other great musicians.

How do we study great musicians? 1) Listen to what is being performed. 2) Transcribe what is being performed. 3) Practice the transcription in its original form. 4) Learn the transcription of the performance in every key or possible application it could be used in.

This is the way great musicians study and become better. The key to being able to effectively study other great musicians is using music theory to understand their musical choices.

Yes, you can just stack notes or take one part of something and stick it somewhere else to make it fit or sound good. However, it is more beneficial to you as a musician to confidently know why something would work. Musically, it is less beneficial for you to be required to guess if something would work. In any music environment, your lack of knowledge and study of the craft will be exposed, namely, when around other creative people who can feel your poor confidence in production. Because you have not done the work to study your musical craft, nor are you open to receiving more knowledge, you position yourself to be the potential cause of a musical derailment. Learning and studying music theory is the initial path you should take in operating in the spirit of excellence of developing your musical craft.

King Solomon is the richest man who ever walked the Earth in the Bible. He was not only rich in gold, talent, and silver, but he also had relationship alliances with powerful countries. In addition to that, Solomon was one of the wisest men to ever walk the Earth. He wrote the Book of Proverbs,

Ecclesiastes, and Song of Songs. He ruled one of the Earth's greatest nations and taught people how to do what he did. There is a Queen of Sheba who comes to visit to see what all the gossip is about concerning Solomon. King Solomon tells her about what he's got going on and what God has shown him to do, and how she can do the same for her land. After King Solomon and the Queen of Sheba take a tour of Solomon's nation, she was able to see how Solomon's servants were dressed. The Queen of Sheba took note of the detail in the decoration of the campus. The Queen was able to encounter an unmatched experience being served at a high level. The Queen of Sheba interrupts Solomon mid-sentence to say, I heard about you and how good you were, but what I have heard and your wisdom is not nearly even half as good as the experience I've gotten here today. The Queen of Sheba paid Solomon 120 talents of gold, an abundance of spices, and precious stones for the experience she encountered with him.

Because King Solomon overdelivered on the experience of his client, she gave him a record number of money, resources, and a long-lasting relationship alliance that allowed other clients to reach out to Solomon for the same solution. When you overdeliver on your experience with clients, businesses, and partnerships, being the creative solution they need, you not only open up the spiritual gateway for an unlimited increase of wealth, but also, you unlock the Earthly access to wealth.

People don't remember what you played, sang, or wrote. Nobody can accurately recall every detail of your performance or production. If they could, they would be you. However, what people remember about you most is how you showed up.

So, when you show up, the way you deliver your message is what produces an abundance of spiritual, emotional, and financial wealth. How you operate in the spirit of excellence is what opens the doors for your wealth to be sustained. While financial wealth is what we desire, if we do not position ourselves spiritually *first* and do the work to create an awareness of emotions, we place limitations on our financial capacity. So, while financial wealth may be the ultimate goal, music creatives must be willing to take intentional time to remove themselves from the craft and shape their spiritual relationship with God *first*.

You have to be willing to step away from your instrument, computer, desk, pen, microphone, etc. You have to be willing to remove yourself from the music environment in order to increase yourself. As a music creative, you must be in the correct state of mind to produce something great. We can be gifted to create while simultaneously seeking balance in our life; however, the pain we experience will at some point begin to reflect in what we create. It is important to be honest with yourself, community, and clients about when you are in a mental position to produce well or not. If you are not, do not force yourself to be creative. Your sadness, doubt, fear, anxiety, and pain will embed itself into your production. When you are ready to produce again, *then* communicate your disinclination and preparation to move forward.

Do not chase money when you are not mentally prepared to receive the abundance of income. At times, we complete projects and accept gigs in order to sustain financial income; however, if we are not mentally prepared to receive, we risk missing opportunities to multiply our finances due to emotional imbalance. When we are sad, depressed, grieving, or even angry, we are more likely to make financial decisions based on 1) removing the need to make a decision quickly or 2) seeking to satisfy our emotional state. We have to create a mental capacity to create music when we are free. This also means that in a season of focus, we must position our finances to allow us the capacity to take time and reposition ourselves. When you do not have the capacity to produce due to stagnation in your emotional state, you limit your creativity to not being able to reach its fullest potential.

Social media and world culture have placed pressure to create mindlessly. Because we want daily content, followers, and views, we spend most of our time curating quantity of content instead of quality of content. As a music creative, this is dangerous because when consumers go to consume your library of reference, they are not experiencing your fullest creativity within each project, song, album, EP, or chart you release. On the other end of things, some music creatives spend too long waiting to release projects and content.

When sound is produced, it is only multiplied by a catalyst that ensures the initial vibration is recreated and amplified. There is little to no time for a sound to exist if an additional vibration has not caused a cycle to form. What am I saying? When you receive a musical idea, there is a limited time to your ability to take that idea and produce it. Lyrically and sonically, it is important to explore the idea and release it to be consumed so that the relevance remains reproduced and amplified by the people who consume it. Sonically, you will miss your moment and people will not be served a message that releases them from pain if you wait too long to release your work. This is why you must remain in a constant spiritual, emotional, and financial position to produce, so that there are no limitations to you being able to release your creative work at any moment necessary.

For those who say, well, what if I need more time? What if I need to work on it some more? What if it's not quite how I want it to sound?

While sounding good and being of high quality are important and a necessary component for people to receive more effectively, if the message of your creative work is clear and aligned with the human need to thrive in any area, it will be received and multiplied openly. You do not need to have a perfect record or score. However, you must be ready to release your work when people need it most. Ultimately, your work is not for you. The creative work you develop to build financial wealth should be designed to help and serve others. If you consistently operate in the spirit of excellence in all that you do, the quality of your creative work will already be of high quality and production, whether it has been fine-tuned or not. If your work is not ready, that exposes a gap in the spiritual, emotional, and financial preparation of yourself and the people you have produced and created with.

Balance is overrated. There are seasons when you must focus in one area in order to be able to have the results from that season of focus work in your favor later. If you are balanced, it is a testament of your seasons of focus. Your balance is a direct result of you taking the time to ensure that you can have the things that you want. However, you must be stretched to capacity in specific areas during certain seasons in order to build the balance around you. I like to think of it as a fresh rubber band. If you stretch a fresh rubber band in one direction, it will pop. If you stretch it in another direction, it may not pop immediately, but it will eventually. However, if you stretch a fresh rubber band in one area then retract, stretch in another area, then retract, stretch it in a third area then retract and repeat the process, when you go to increase the entire size of the rubber band it will not break, because there was intentional time spent to ensure there was an elastic capacity in multiple areas. The same theory applies to our life. We have to be willing to be stretched in multiple areas for a moment of time, so that when it is time for us to expand, we are balanced in every area, thus having the capacity for an effective and sustained growth.

Innovation

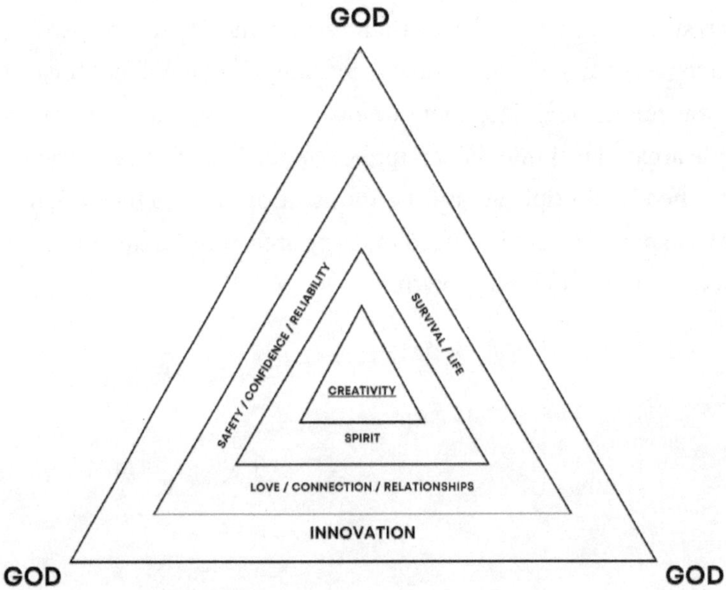

This is the biggest message of this book. In order to create wealth from your creative gift, you must consult with the spirit of God *first* to define the direction you are spiritually assigned and graced to write and produce in. From then, continue to consult with God about every decision you make and experience you encounter. This continued consultation with God is for clarity on the message you should be telling to the specific community God wants you to serve. From then, use that message consistently to build a platform and develop offers to serve that community and set them free based on the principles of God's order according to the Bible.

If you remember nothing from this book. What you have just read is the most important piece of information that is going to guarantee you going from just being creative and talented to thriving in emotional, financial, and spiritual wealth *from* being creative and talented.

If you never step away from the creative center and begin to activate your ideas in the areas of focus God has presented us with, you will stay lost. You are lost because you never created an avenue to innovate your creativity. In other words, at some point, you have to actually do the thing. You have to actually do the creative thing you have in your mind. The reason you have to actually do the creative thing is because there are parts of your creative process that must innovate. You have to release your creative work so that you are able to create a reflection for improvement.

What is interesting in the way God designed us is that we can see everything and everybody except for ourselves. In order for us to see ourselves, there must be a catalyst in place to serve as a reflection of our existence. The creative work we release is the catalyst. The outcome we receive is the reflection. The only way we can innovate beyond creativity is by allowing the creative gift we have to produce a body of work that can be innovated and grow to its fullest potential.

Innovation is at the outer layer of the areas of focus within The Legacy Order ™, because innovating what we create and what has been created in different areas of life is how we move cultures, industries, and nations forward. While creating new ideas is necessary, if we never innovate what already exists, we miss the opportunity to grow what is already good. In Genesis, God declares that his creations are good; however, Adam was able to increase, grow, expand, and move an entire culture and industry by taking what God made good and making it better. Because the industry is oversaturated with negative emotions based on lack, our responsibility as spiritually aligned believers is to take the narratives of industry music and innovate them to be creative works that not only validate emotions but also serve people by providing a strategy to heal and thrive.

Don't be the person who has a lot of creativity but nobody knows. Don't be the person that is very creative but no one is aware because it is all in your head. You have to release your creative work.

Some may say, Well, I'm holding on to my ideas until I'm ready to release them, because I don't want anybody to take my stuff. You're trying to build a vocabulary of work without releasing anything because you want to create a master project of your creativity. While honoring your confidentiality is important, having people consume large quantities of your creative work can be overbearing. It's like a friend telling you they can cook very well. They finally invite you for dinner, and there are over 30 dishes that they have prepared for you to try. While every dish may be well prepared, tasteful, and something you like, you are highly unlikely to consume all with the greatest enjoyment within one setting because it is simply too much to take in. No, don't spend an entire creative career releasing singles and clips of songs; however, create musical works that display your creativity in a unified light. At times your light will shine fully, other times your light will shine bright, and other times your light will have color; however, if you present people with every color of your creativity at once, none of them can be consumed effectively.

Additionally, don't be afraid to release your creation because you believe someone will take your work. When you are creative and good at how you express your creativity, someone will always imitate you. By imitating you, what they are doing is trying to connect with the power and ability within yourself to open opportunities for them. People are going to innovate your work and make it better for their benefit. The reason we feel threatened by this narrative is because we have not positioned ourselves to receive and multiply the creativity we release beyond it just being something we worked on. We feel threatened because we have not gone beyond just creating for fun. With everything that we produce, there must be a planned outcome that allows us to multiply our financial increase. We are threatened by people who may potentially steal our creative ideas because we are still on the same level as the people who will take from us. We have not created a plan to innovate our creativity for the purpose of financial gain. So, we are fighting with the creatives who can only take ideas because we have not created a market for our creativity to produce more for us on its own. In order to win and beat this narrative, you have to elevate yourself and release your creative work with stronger intent. Your creative work must serve a purpose and people beyond sounding good.

We have the power to be creative. Which means, no one can produce how we produce. When we operate at our fullest creative potential and innovation, there is no one who can recreate what we do. If we are worried that someone else does have the power to recreate what we do, we must innovate ourselves to ensure we are set apart. We must innovate and improve our creative craft to define a clear difference between us and those who are able to do what we do. It is not arrogant to clearly define that our ability cannot be replicated. You can settle in accepting that you are a creative who imitates and never pushes the narrative forward; however, that mindset is inseparable from the acceptance that you are not reaching your fullest spiritual, emotional, and financial potential. And in so, you are in disobedience of God's will to have abundance in your life and beyond. The innovation we create must serve other people.

Moreover, why would God give two people the same instructions? It is because the way we are meant to express and who we are called to serve is different. Even if you believe that your creativity is not strong, know that you are being selfish if you are not releasing what is needed to serve other people. It is so crucial for you to release it, because the only way some people understand and become free is through the way you communicate. Your unique life experiences allow you to communicate with a specific community of people. Imagine if I refused to write this book. How selfish of me would it be to write this information and never release it? It is not fair to myself, you, and many other readers to hold information and communication that can set someone free and ignite their path of creating spiritual, emotional, and financial wealth.

God

The covenant of our legacy is with God. In The Legacy Order ™, God is the covering source of all of our being and existence. God just needs you to obey because He already knows you can be trusted with His voice. God leads you in a way that lets everything fall into place at the exact moment it needs to, instead of showing you the whole picture at once. If God revealed every detail of your life today, you would either get overwhelmed, tap out too early, or try to rush and fix what was never broken. The truth is that God works in timing. His timing builds the spiritual, emotional, and financial abundance He promised you. His timing is what opens the space for miracles to actually manifest.

About the Author

Brandon is an author, entrepreneur, musician, and mentor—"Brandon" to friends and "UncleBrandon" to just about everyone else. With a professional foundation in Social Work and a passion for ministry, he has built a platform dedicated to empowerment and practical transformation.

Through AskUncleBrandon, he helps musicians, artists, and creative entrepreneurs establish their business structure so they can grow their vision with stability and a real plan. UncleBrandon's work bridges the gap between purpose and profitability, teaching creatives how to build sustainable businesses without losing their spiritual identity or their artistic voice.

As the host of the LifeLock Podcast, Brandon leads honest conversations about family, finances, faith, and the transitions that shape us. Whether he is mentoring artists, consulting music creatives, performing, speaking, or serving in ministry, Brandon's mission remains the same:

When equipped with the right tools and anchored by faith, anyone can transform their gift into a lasting legacy.

www.ingramcontent.com/pod-product-compliance
Lightning Source LLC
LaVergne TN
LVHW100315210926
848480LV00003B/1127
* 9 7 9 8 2 1 8 8 8 7 4 6 9 *